Lecture Notes in Computer Science 1028
Edited by G. Goos, J. Hartmanis and J. van Leeuwen

Springer
Berlin
Heidelberg
New York
Barcelona
Budapest
Hong Kong
London
Milan
Paris
Santa Clara
Singapore
Tokyo

Nabil R. Adam Yelena Yesha (Eds.)

Electronic Commerce

Current Research Issues and Applications

Springer

Volume Editors

Nabil R. Adam
Computing and Information Systems
MS/CIS Department, Rutgers University
180 University Avenue, Newark, NJ 07102, USA

Yelena Yesha
Computer Science Department
University of Maryland Baltimore County
Baltimore, MD 21228-5398, USA

Cataloging-in-Publication data applied for

Die Deutsche Bibliothek - CIP-Einheitsaufnahme

Electronic commerce : current research issues and applications / Nabil R. Adam ; Yelena Yesha (ed.). - Berlin ; Heidelberg ; New York ; Barcelona ; Budapest ; Hong Kong ; London ; Milan ; Paris ; Santa Clara ; Singapore ; Tokyo : Springer, 1996
(Lecture notes in computer science ; 1028)
ISBN 3-540-60738-2
NE: Adam, Nabil R. [Hrsg.]; GT

CR Subject Classification (1991): H.4, H.5, J.1, J.4, K.4.1, K.5.1-2, K.6.5, D.4.6

ISBN 3-540-60738-2 Springer-Verlag Berlin Heidelberg New York

Typesetting: Camera-ready by author
SPIN 10512384 06/3142 – 5 4 3 2 1 0 Printed on acid-free paper

Preface

A workshop was held at the National Institute of Standards and Technology in Gaithersburg, Maryland on December 1, 1994. The workshop provided an international forum to discuss evolving research issues and applications in the area of Electronic Commerce. Invited speakers from industry, universities, and government presented their experiences and visions for the future. Researchers from the U.S. and from several other countries including Australia, The Netherlands, and Ireland participated in the workshop.

Nabil R. Adam and Yelena Yesha served as the program co-chairs. The workshop resulted in several papers that were reviewed, and their final versions are included in this book. We would like to express our deep personal thanks to the program committee members and the reviewers for their constructive comments and suggestions. In addition, Nabil Adam would like to thank Dr. Shamim Naqvi of Bellcore for his support and help in this project, and also acknowledge the support he received during the preparation of this book from the Center of Excellence in Space Data and Information Sciences (CESDIS) at the NASA Goddard Space Flight Center.

Nabil R. Adam
Yelena Yesha

September 1995

Contents

Chapter 1

Overview

Nabil R. Adam[1] and Yelena Yesha[2]

The first chapter provides an introduction and background discussion on electronic commerce. This is followed by a chapter that addresses issues related to adoption of Electronic Data Interchange (EDI) into electronic commerce. The adoption of EDI into electronic commerce has been much slower than expected. The second chapter of the book discusses some of the obstacles in adopting EDI into electronic commerce and shows that by modifying the standards approach to flexible messaging overcomes most of these obstacles and makes it very easy for business to move ahead.

UN/EDIFACT and ANSI/X12 are enormous standards for commercial electronic transaction formats, originally based on business forms. Their serious drawbacks have prevented most businesses from using them and have made it very expensive to combine EDI with the relevant information systems within a business. The current standards have no machine-usable semantic definitions, only field-names and some natural language comments. The EDI process of negotiating a different electronic trading agreement for each trading partner is too burdensome. The EDI message syntax is an unnecessary nuisance, but the semantic categories collected in the standards are valuable distillations of real commercial practice.

The next chapter proposes that EDI is a special case of the semantic data integration problem, and to solve this a proposal is made for formal conceptual definitions of all data elements and codes, using the basic "ontologies" constructed within the AI field. The chapter also describes a machine-negotiation mechanism by which two trading partners with no prior human negotiation can establish common ontologies, syntax formats, communication channels and legal obligations. They can then commence trading immediately. So defined, EDI could be integrated automatically with other systems and standards. Various specific possibilities are surveyed.

Law has given a prompt response to the innovations that EDI has introduced

[1]Rutgers University, Newark, NJ 07102, Email: adam@adam.rutgers.edu

[2]Computer Science Department, University of Maryland Baltimore County, Baltimore, MD 21228-5398, and Center of Excellence in Space Data and Information Sciences, Email: yeyesha@cs.umbc.edu

in trade practices. This has taken the form of model agreements among trade partners which address the crucial issues of the interchange. However to what extent do the model agreements reflect new developments such as open EDI? Are the model agreements widely used in their present form? What aspect would trade partners seek to modify in order to protect their interests? To what extent can a trade partner with a dominant position in the market dictate its opinion on its counterpart? Furthermore, there are some competition issues that trade partners should consider when they deal with EDI. Are interchange agreements adequate for the regulation of EDI issues, or should there be another approach to them, such as a Code of Practice or a binding model agreement. In Chapter four of the book a discussion of these issues is presented.

The following chapter describes the design of an EDI audit and control workbench which integrates EDI and workflow technologies to provide a system that tracks routing, authorization and logging of a document from it's production to it's transmission to a trading partner by electronic means. The focus is on the security aspects of the workbench. A scheme involving a novel application of IBM's control vector technology is outline. This allows an individual who is authorized to sign trade documents below a certain maximum value to collaborate with his/her peers to amplify this signing power. Two distinct schemes are described, one for centralized organizations, and another involving the use of secure hardware devices which allows the scheme to be effected in a more distributed environment.

The current healthcare environment of consolidation and cost cutting is creating loosely coupled groups termed "virtual healthcare enterprises". In order to control costs, manage information, and provide seamless care, these enterprises will benefit from electronic commerce: electronic distribution of many transaction types, including clinical, administrative, and financial. In this context, automated workflow: automating the flow of documents and related information through a business process may be viewed as an essential component of electronic commerce. The next chapter discuss the development of tools for acquiring, representing, and simulating workflow for healthcare enterprises. This was part of a multi-year project within a multiple-site consortium called HOST (Healthcare Open Systems and Trials). Lacking in current workflow tools is the crucial ability to model and track the time resources of tasks within an overall process. In this chapter explicit temporal reasoning for automated workflow is advocated and demonstrated. It is further shown as to how temporal models of some healthcare processes may provide valuable information to clinicians, administrators, and patients.

The information marketplace is on the horizon. However, it is unlikely that the basic functions of commerce will appreciably change even as the coming electronic revolution dramatically changes the forms of commerce. Thus, it is important to carefully consider existing commercial activities in designing and proposing new infrastructures for the future. The last chapter of the book assesses the needs of business providers with respect to the information marketplace, and proposes a four-part solution to meeting those needs: (1) a facilitation layer based on the notion of multiple cooperating agents, (2) a functional access language to provide mechanized access to provider agents, (3) an interface description language to provide consumers with manual access to providers, and (4) a series of special facilitation agents that provide operations support for commercial activities.

Chapter 2

Electronic Commerce: An Overview[1]

Nabil R. Adam[2] and Yelena Yesha[3]

2.1 Introduction

In a narrow sense Electronic commerce can be defined as the process of conducting commercial transactions, which are done today through various media such as paper, phone, and fax *electronically* without prior arrangements. In this sense, Electronic Commerce supports traditional commercial models in which consumers acquire, analyze and decide on their commercial actions as in the traditional, mostly manual, case. Only certain aspects of their commercial decisions are supported electronically. A simple example of this definition of Electronic Commerce is paying for a purchase through a credit card in which the credit card transaction is handled electronically.

However, as the world is brought closer together by internetworking and more and more information becomes available in an online manner, we find that consumers are spending more and more of their time on the electronic medium. Conceptually, there is no difference between a consumer spending time in a physical shopping mall and spending time browsing an electronic shopping mall. Thus, the electronic medium is as viable a medium of conducting commerce as any other medium. It has some limitations and some strengths, just like any other medium. It is to be fully expected that the electronic medium will spawn the same kinds of commercial activities as other media.

In this sense Electronic Commerce (EC) can be defined as the entire collection of actions that support commercial activities on a network. These activities spawn product information and display actions, services (e.g., finding more information about certain products), providers, consumers, advertizers, electronic malls, support for transactions, brokering systems for a variety of services and

[1] We would like to thank Shamim Naqvi for his valuable comments on an earlier draft of this chapter

[2] Rutgers University, Center for Information Management, Integration and Connectivity, 180 University Avenue, Newark, NJ 07102, Email: adam@adam.rutgers.edu

[3] Computer Science Department, University of Maryland Baltimore County, Baltimore, MD 21228-5398, and Center of Excellence in Space Data and Information Sciences, Email: yeyesha@cs.umbc.edu

actions (e.g., finding certain products, finding cheaply priced products, etc), security of transactions, user authentication, etc.

If indeed our social structures are becoming more and more oriented towards electronic information, as is evidenced by the strong interest in Internet and the Information Super Highway, there will be continual strong demand for EC activities on the information networks. Many commercial organizations have already anticipated this trend, and have strong market presence on some of the networks. Various companies are offering a large collection of products and product information on the Internet, and commercial transactions are currently flowing on the Internet. The government itself has shown interest in supporting EC on information networks.

2.2 Requirements and Services

An electronic commerce system has to satisfy a set of requirements and provide users with a set of services including the following:

- *Information Repositories.* An EC system must contain information repository on the various products and services in the system. Vendors should be able to add and modify new and existing products and services, and consumers should be able to access what is available. This does not imply that the EC system contains central repositories of product/service information. Individual vendors may be the keepers and maintainers of their own repositories. The system, however, must contain in a centralized and/or distributed manner various information resources on products and services. For example, several efforts have concentrated on providing online catalogs of product and service information. Such catalogs are usually provided one or more well-defined vendors who publicize and list their products in the catalogs. Other efforts have concentrated on providing yellow page directory systems for product and service information. The purpose of such systems is to be a vendor-independent directory of product and services. Yellow page directories are also provided for consumers and vendors.

  Coupled with information repositories, an EC system must also allow consumers to act on the information that the system contains. For example, consumers must be able to complete transactions on products and services if they so desire and if the providers support such a model of interactivity. The central issue here is whether EC supports an efficient market? By an efficient market we mean a market in which the consumer is assured of finding a product or service that fits exactly some metric or specification, e.g., cheapest price for a given product. Traditional markets are no efficient in this sense: consumers have no such guarantees and in fact finding a reasonable product or service may involve considerable leg work. An EC system must support both models of markets, the efficient model and and the inefficient model of markets. In some cases, vendors may simply want to conclude the interaction by having the consumers know about the product and/or the service. In other cases, a vendor may supply all the details about a product or service and expect the consumer to make a decision based on that information.

- *Finding services and products.* How do consumers find products and services? In a network, consumers will need online facilities that not only help them in locating resources but also provide help in locating resources that match certain expectations and desires. For example, brokering systems may be used to find products within certain price ranges. Matchmaking programs will bring together producers and consumers. Example of such a service include:

  - Mechanisms to describe information services by capability rather than name.
  - Mechanisms to perform content-based routing.
  - Methods to integrate various search engines.

  Gateway services will allow consumers to locate resources across multiple networks.

- *Electronic analogs of current financial instruments.* Mechanisms for billing customers and receiving payment from customers are among the basic requirements of the system. Examples of financial instruments include bidding, purchase orders, digital cash, extension of credit. Emphasis will be provided by billing services. What are the consumers billed for when they use a service? Is it based on the time they use a service, or the particular features of the service? Consumers in fact may not purchase objects in an EC system but may decide to "lease" resources. All of these issues point to many faceted billing systems.

- *Security.* On one hand the system must be secure against malicious use, misuse and data-corruption failure and must ensure that the privacy of its users as well as the intellectual property of the vendors are protected. On the other hand, however, the system should provide open access so that vendors can add/update information and services any time. Authentication and security services such as privacy, authentication, integrity, confidentiality, authorization, and controls.

- *Format Conversion and Data Interchange.* Conversion services to promote interoperation is an essential service. Examples of such a service include support interoperation among different Electronic Data Interchange (EDI) standards and other electronic forms.

Most electronic commerce transactions today are done using dedicated lines and over value-added networks. These media ease security issues but make open access harder. An interesting question is whether electronic commerce should be done over the Internet? On one hand, the Internet supports open access, has over 20 million users worldwide, and experiences an enormous growth rate. On the other hand, however, the Internet in its current state has some shortcomings, including

- It is largely insecure although secure versions of several protocols are being considered.
- Most protocols do not have quality of service guarantees or have minimal quality of service guarantees.
- It is difficult to locate resources, largely relying on the browsing capability of consumers. However, many new search engines are quickly coming online.
- It does not have mechanisms to protect intellectual property.
- It is highly heterogeneous.

The medium of choice must promote an open marketplace of services and information, be trusted, provide financial services, and protect intellectual property.

2.3 Potential Benefits from Electronic Commerce

We have argued above that the electronic media has strengths and weaknesses like other media as far as commercial activities are concerned. In this sense, it is meaningless to compare its commercial benefits. For example, TV, radio and newspapers provide different media for advertizing and each has its own strengths and weaknesses. One can, however, argue that the electronic media possesses certain inherent advantages. These include

- Procurement processes can be streamlined and trading procedures can be standardized through computerization.
- Delays and errors in procurement can be reduced. The transmission speed and ability to check human errors of electronic commerce environments reduce possible delays and errors.
- Cut overall costs via more competitive procurement. The electronic commerce environments provide more efficient and informative market places for matchmaking and competition.
- Decrease length of product development cycles. Product development cycles can be shortened via more competitive markets and more efficient supply channels.

- Enable enterprises to conduct business with distant partners the same way they do with neighboring partners. In other words, geographical neighborhood becomes meaningless and producers can partner more effectively based on more fundamental principles such as product matches.

- Empower small businesses. EC will empower small businesses via providing more equal opportunity to access and exchange information in marketplaces. ' Very large corporations are finding it very difficult to design a viable Internet presence whereas the companies who seem to have strong presence and strong marketing and products are the smaller companies. This also again confirms the belief that electronic networks provide a different medium for Electronic Commerce for which newer business and commercial models will need to be developed.

- Create new services and businesses. Some business that originally can not provide certain services due to distant or less efficient marketplace can now provide their services. Again, since electronic networks will need new business models, many new opportunities will be provided to new players through these models.

- Lead to leaner and more competitive economy.

2.4 Information Integration

Currently, the electronic commerce environment has the following characteristics:

- Massive volumes of data. As a result of the U.S. government initiative to support the development of an enhanced information infrastructure and rapid advances in computer and communication technologies, we now have a global information system. A large number of heterogeneous information sources are available on the Internet.

- Browsing as standard access paradigm. As the interfaces, search mechanisms, and index methods are not expected to be standardized, browsing is the standard access paradigm instead of use a set of criteria to inquiry.

- Unintegrated search engines. Search engines available can be keyword-based, ontology-based, content-based, etc. These search engines are not integrated or collaborative.

- Heterogeneous structures. The information sources available are designed, maintained, and contributed by enterprises in various industries to provide different services. As a result, the electronic commerce marketplaces contain services which are heterogeneous in structures, formats, access methods, and quality of the services. The mismatch found in autonomously developed resources and services, ranges from platforms, operating systems, database systems and models, data representations, ontology, semantics, and processing paradigms.

- Proprietary and/or incompatible services. Because of massive volumes of data and browsing as a major access paradigm, the process of matchmaking may not be effective (no service) or efficient (incompatible services, time consuming, or expensive).
- Legacy systems. Legacy systems are pre-existing or autonomous resources, not designed to interoperate within a general and flexible architecture. These legacy systems may not be able to directly interoperate with some other open systems that are designed more recently.

The consequences of such an environment are:

- Unused information. Available information can not well utilized.
- Misinformed decisions. Decisions are not made based on available information resources but information can be accessed within reasonable search time.
- More manual processing. Browsing is the major access method. The search process is usually tedious and basically a manual process.
- Increased delays and costs. If the electronic commerce environment can not serve as a match-making market place effectively and efficiently in time and cost, it only causes increased delays and costs compared to current traditional trading methods.

Such an EC environment raises several questions, including

- There is several different kinds of heterogeneity in network information systems. How can such heterogeneity of the networks be resolved? Possibilities exist in mapping through domain-specific ontologies or machine learning techniques.
  - Lexical differences. Naming problems encountered here are that synonyms occur when objects with different names represent the same concepts, and homonyms occur when the names are the same but different concepts are represented. Synonyms are resolved by consulting a synonym lexicon while a domain-specific ontology are necessary to identify homonyms.
  - Structural differences. Structural heterogeneity occurs since the participating information sources are designed individually, A data item may be designed as an entity while it may be designed as an attribute.
  - Semantic differences. It occurs when there is a disagreement about the meaning, interpretation, or intended use of the same or related data. We argued that identifying semantically related objects and then resolving the schematic differences is the *fundamental* question in any approach to information system interoperability.

- What to do with legacy systems?
  - Development of interfaces. One option is interoperable systems by putting a new, standard interface on existing systems. It preserves the data in existing systems, yet uses it in new interoperable systems. This transforms the existing systems into open ones. Interoperability allows computing resources to be shared.
  - Development of wrappers. This approach uses wrapper and surround technology tools which adapt legacy resources to conform with access standards and conventions used in mediation and coordination.
  - Devise strategies to migrate to new systems. In migration or reengineering, the application logic, data definition, and data itself in those old systems are lifted and transferred into a new, replacement system. The advantage of this approach is that the new systems are easier to maintain. However, this process is usually too expensive.
- How to enable users to manage massive information spaces?
  - Mechanisms to describe contributed and requested information. The dominant computer paradigm will involve a large number of information sources that are heterogeneous in semantics and format. Automatically extracting and understanding the semantics of information and format conversion are important issues to information integration and such metadata should be based on the contents of the information available.
  - Mechanisms to express evaluation methods and to request evaluations. Evaluation methods are essential to assist users to manage massive information space. Evaluation methods need to provide functions such as filtering to improve relevance of query content information, ranking to assign values to retrieved content objects and explanation.
  - Coordinate mechanisms. Need mechanisms to collaborate mediators, coordinate domain-specific knowledge and merge ontology.
  - Mechanisms to create taxonomies.
  - Methods to perform feature extraction and to summarize multimedia information resources. It is necessary to develop mechanisms to extract features (signatures) from multimedia information resources and present them as metadata which can later be used to index and retrieve non-text information.

2.5 Examples of Specific Projects

Several electronic commerce related projects are currently underway. Examples of such projects, include:

- Internet Shopping Centers (supporting browsing as the standard access method).
- Electronic cash developed by DigiCash. It enables users to have electronic-money signed by a bank.
- CyberCash develops tools that enable users to interact with their banks.

It is important to note, however that, to our knowledge, none of these projects supports untraceable secure digital cash of many denominations yet.

2.5.1 G-7 Project: Global Market Place for Small and Medium Enterprises

In addition to the above mentioned projects, a major project that has just begun is the collaboration among the US and the G-7 countries on the development and demonstration of an electronic commerce pilot implementation that will rapidly and significantly increase industrial efficiency and global trade.

The following are example Projects to be undertaken:

- Expand the CommerceNet/NIST (National Institute of Standards and Technology) Smart Procurement demonstration into a full fledged pilot for competitive global procurement.
- Support Internet EDI, particularly government and private global trade facilitation services.
- Develop a pilot implementation to demonstrate a manufacturing environment for product development and supply chain management using the STEP standard for exchange of product data, IGES, CAD systems, etc.
- Support internationalization of the Department of Defense sponsored Continuous Acquisition Lifecycle Support (CALS) program.
- Develop directory services for resources on the global information infrastructure (GII)

Chapter 3

The Standardisation of Flexible EDI Messages

Ken Steel[1]

3.1 Introduction

Electronic Commerce is the business of transacting business electronically - the "paperless office".

There are at least two parties to a business transaction; one party is said to initiate the transaction [the initiator] and the other party or parties respond to that initiative [the responder(s)]. A transaction necessarily involves the flow of information between these parties [Data Interchange].

There are four classes of electronic interface over which data can be interchanged in the course of transacting business: human-to-human, human-to-machine, machine-to-human and machine-to-machine.

Human-to-human interchanges can involve voice communications or facsimile; such communication need not be highly structured and must be interpreted by a human to enable action to be taken. Human-to-machine involves the human initiator entering the transaction data directly into a responding application program on a computer by keyboard or other means; this data will be structured in such a way that the application program can interpret and act upon the information received. Machine-to-human involves an initiating computer application program providing information to a human for interpretation and action usually by visualisation (printing on paper or display on a screen) or simulated electronic voice response; as the interpretation will be performed by a human, this information does not need to be highly structured and may contain instructions in "free text" that can only be comprehended and acted upon by a human. Machine-to-machine involves one computer application program producing information that is intended to be interpreted and acted upon by another computer application program without any form of human intervention.

Transacting business across a machine-to-machine interface with no form of human intervention is termed Electronic Data Interchange (EDI).

Electronic Commerce using EDI has been touted over many years as a way to achieve great cost savings and increases in efficiency. Despite this, the rate

[1] The University of Melbourne, Department of Computer Science, 24th November, 1994

at which the technology has been adopted throughout the world has been very slow [73].

A survey of users of EDI was carried out in an attempt to find the reasons for this very poor progress. Section 2 reports the findings of this survey and concludes that the current methods of standardisation are, at best, barely suitable for EDI and Electronic Commerce.

Section 3 examines the way in which applications are designed and operate and finds that a more suitable method of structuring the data for interchange across a machine-to-machine interface which make it easier, faster and less expensive to enable application programs for use with EDI in an Electronic Commerce scenario.

In earlier research where the effects were studied of functionality variations in the interoperating application programs engaged in Electronic Commerce, it was concluded that a method of standardising flexible interchange structures would be desirable and a method proposed [51]. Section 4 refines this new standardisation approach and concludes that it not only produces a true standard for EDI, but also removes a large proportion of the problems of EDI-enabling application programs.

Section 5 relates the usage of the standardisation of flexible messaging to the problems inhibiting the adoption of EDI and Electronic Commerce revealed in the survey of users. It finds that the standardisation of flexible messaging goes a long way towards solving them and in the process, automates the standardisation process. It also determines that the method really produces a true standard.

Section 6 describes a simple and practical method of escaping from the current EDI dilemma and to move a major step forward in an orderly and cost effective way to the new horizons of Electronic Commerce.

Section 7 summarises the benefits of truly standard EDI by this approach and recommends its adoption by the business community.

3.2 A Survey Of EDI Users

Many Industry Working Party Meetings of established and new users of EDI were attended over an eighteen month period. Also during this period, the Working Parties of EDI Software Producers were attended followed by in-depth discussions with application programmers and business systems designers.

This research revealed one dominant reason for this slow adoption of EDI: the great difficulty and cost of achieving interoperation between the application programs involved in the transaction using the current methods of EDI "standardisation".

This stems partly from the tendency for each business to adopt its own proprietary version of a "standard" from the rich selection offered by each of the standards organisations. The word "standard" implies that everyone will do it the same way. This does not appear to be what is happening, thus bringing into question the success of the whole EDI standardisation process.

Other areas of continual discontent reported by experienced users of EDI stem from the bureaucratic standardisation process itself: the tedium and cost of long hours of involvement by senior personnel in working parties agreeing to the way in which a particular version of a selected "standard" will be implemented in that industry grouping (this has to be repeated for each business transaction); having to re-negotiate this agreement every time new businesses join the community; and the extremely drawn out process of achieving a new or modified "standard" which often takes several years. Businesses are both unwilling and unable to be put on hold for this length of time.

But the major reason appears to be that current methods of standardisation of the structure of data being interchanged across a machine-to-machine interface totally ignore the way in which applications and programs are designed and operated.

The software producers saw the problems from a different perspective. They cited the extreme complexity of the current standards and their unwillingness to invest the very substantial time and training to enable their staff to gain sufficient competence to properly EDI-enable their packaged applications.

When the role of translators was explained, the general consensus was that the cheaper translators their customers buy are not able to fully map to their application programs. The standardisation process seems totally absorbed in building "standard" messages or transaction sets as an end in itself instead of a means of achieving interoperation between initiating and responding application programs.

It could be said, therefore, that the current methods of EDI standardisation are less than suitable for EDI and for use in Electronic Commerce. Whether the result is really a standard is also highly questionable.

3.3 Examining Commercial Applications

In the previous section it was discovered that the major obstacles preventing the widespread adoption of EDI for Electronic Commerce stems from the lack of consideration of the design and operation of application programs in the current EDI standardisation process.

This section examines firstly the way application programs operate in processing a business transaction; then the way they are constructed for standalone operation is then examined and finally, how they can be converted for interoperation with other programs for the purposes of Electronic Commerce.

As a result of this examination, a very simple way of structuring the data being interchanged between the interoperating applications is discovered. Not only does it simplify and reduce the cost of EDI-enablement of application programs, but also markedly reduces the amount of data that needs to be interchanged and is more powerful in preserving the context of the data.

The initiating application program engaged in Electronic Commerce usually proceeds as follows:

- The database for the particular business system is referenced in some way and information extracted from it.

- The data to be interchanged is assembled and transported to the responding application program of the trading partner.

The data to be interchanged is either directly extracted from or derived from the relational context of the business system's database prior to being assembled into the interchange structure by the initiating application program.

The responding application program essentially does exactly the reverse: reads the incoming data and posts it to the business system's database.

The data in most business databases these days are organised according to the relationships with other elements of data according to a procedure known as "third normal form" (3NF) [51]. Since data originating from the initiating application comes directly or indirectly from a database, it will probably be organised in 3NF. When the responding program receives the data, it posts it directly or indirectly to another database - also usually in 3NF. There, application programs would be required to provide the minimum of data manipulation capability if the data being interchanged were also in 3NF.

Consider a purchasing transaction.

The initiating application program works through the stock and determines what should be re-ordered based on a set of business rules. Having decided how many at how much from which supplier, the purchase requisitions are posted to the database. After an approval process (which may be totally electronic), the purchase requisitions are sent to the appropriate trading partners as purchase orders. The appropriate view of the database is shown in figure 1. Note the classes from which data is drawn: Suppliers, Purchase orders, Stock on order, stock location and products.

On receipt of the purchase orders, the responding application program checks stock levels and prices and then distributes the information across a database similar to that shown in figure 2. From the database are produced picking slips, invoices, serial shipping container labels and advance shipping notices.

Comparing the databases used by the initiator and the responder in a purchasing transaction shows a very similar relational distribution of data. Moving the data between the application programs according to these classes should be a lot simpler than twisting it around to an electronic simulation of a paper-based document and then converting it back to the original context at the other end.

It would therefore appear more efficient and practical to build an interchange structure where each segment contained the appropriate data from each class of the database used in the business transaction. This would reduce the number of segments in a Purchasing Interchange Structure from the maximum of 157 used in the EDIFACT "orders" message to a maximum of 12 if not translated to EDIFACT and presented instead in 3NF.

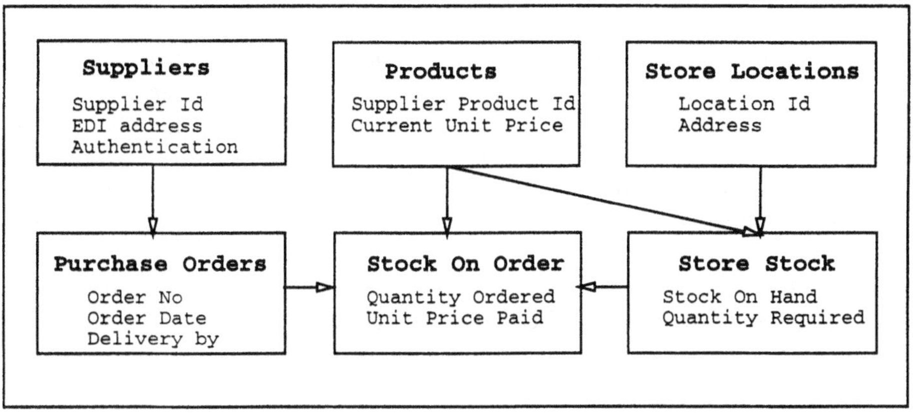

Figure 3.1 Purchase Order View

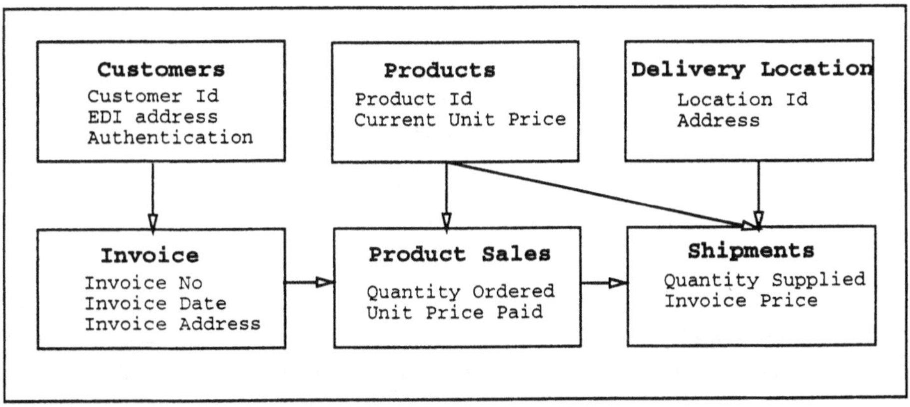

Figure 3.2 Customer Order View

3.4 Refining Flexible Message Standards

If the principles developed in the previous section were adopted where each segment in the interchange structure were composed of data elements from a particular database class, then the segment structure within the message (transaction set) would vary with the relational structure of the database. Variations could therefore be expected between the interchange structure generated by the initiating application program and the expectation of the responding application program.

In previous research, the effect of application program functionality on the data interchange structure has been studied [73] and a solution to the standardisation of variable interchange structures proposed.

3.4.1 Handling the Interchange Structure

The basic principles of the proposed method of standardising flexible interchange structures are as follows:

1. An EDIFACT message called ICSDEF describes the structure of the data produced or required by an application program.

2. The programmer who writes (or modifies) the initiating application program describes the structure of the data it produces in an ICSDEF message.

3. The programmer who writes (or modifies) the responding application program describes the structure of the data it expects in an ICSDEF message.

4. Both parties use a new-breed translator called an EDI Server which automates the standardisation approach rather than use a burgeoning bureaucracy.

5. The first time the initiator attempts to do business with a particular responder, the EDI Server precedes the raw transaction data straight out of the application program with the ICSDEF describing its structure.

6. The responding EDI Server stores the initiator's ICSDEF in its EDI directory for use each time that same initiator processes the same transaction. This means that the initiator's ICSDEF is only transported on first contact or whenever the initiating application program is changed. The responder's ICSDEF is never transported, but only used locally. (When interactive-edi is introduced, the responder's ICSDEF has to be sent to the initiator so it can decode the response.)

7. The responding EDI Server uses the initiator's ICSDEF to decode the incoming transaction data into individual data elements and uses the ICSDEF for the responding application program to reassemble the data elements into the structure expected by the responding program.

The effect that has been achieved by this approach is to automate the work of the current standards organisations Message Development Groups (MDG) and the Technical Assessment Groups (TAG). Whenever an application program is changed in such a way that the structure of the data being interchanged is affected, the change is implemented instantaneously wherever it applies in a totally standard and automatic way.

In contrast to the rich variety of versions of messages (transaction sets) offered by each of the EDI standards organisations which allows any user to select their own proprietary flavour (and they do), with this new approach there is only one message, ICSDEF, used to describe the interchange structure for each and every business transaction anywhere in the world. This approach, therefore, introduces for the first time, the opportunity for a real world-wide EDI standard. ICSDEF conforms strictly to the EDIFACT syntax as defined in ISO 9735 version 3 and is implemented to ISO 9735 version 4 [80] excluding the Interactive-edi section (which needs a lot more work to be generally implementable).

3.4.2 The Basic Semantic Repository

The ICSDEF message for describing the data written and read by an application program for interchange with the trading partner to process a business transaction is built by the application programmer. The EDI Server at the responding end of the transaction maps the interchange structure from the initiator into the input expected by the responding application. To be able to do this, a consistent label must be applied to each data element to uniquely identify the data it carries, the granularity and its semantics.

This is achieved through a kind of standard data dictionary, termed a Basic Semantic Repository (BSR). The basic concept is very similar to that evolved by the ISO/ECE initiative [11]. The BSR is originally derived from the EDIFACT directory. The semantics of the BSR are then tightened up by hand.

A set of rules is devised by which an English language label (Standard Language Label) for the data element (now called a Basic Semantic Unit or BSU) is derived. The aim of these rules is to produce as close to a unique name for a particular BSR, no matter who does it around the world. Then a Common language label is allocated for use in non-English speaking countries.

Because the BSU may now not be exactly the same as the original EDIFACT data element, not all matches will be exact; some may in fact be described by multiple data elements. References ("Bridges") are built from the BSR back to the appropriate data element(s) in each EDI standards directory in use (figure 3). A more detailed explanation of the derivation, construction and standardisation of the BSR is available in [72].

Labelling and agreeing on the description could easily develop into the same bureaucratic megalith that characterises the administration of the current standardisation procedure. Although the frequency of changes in terms of data elements is much lower than that with transaction sets (messages) in the current standards, and not as time-critical, being able to move ahead with the business

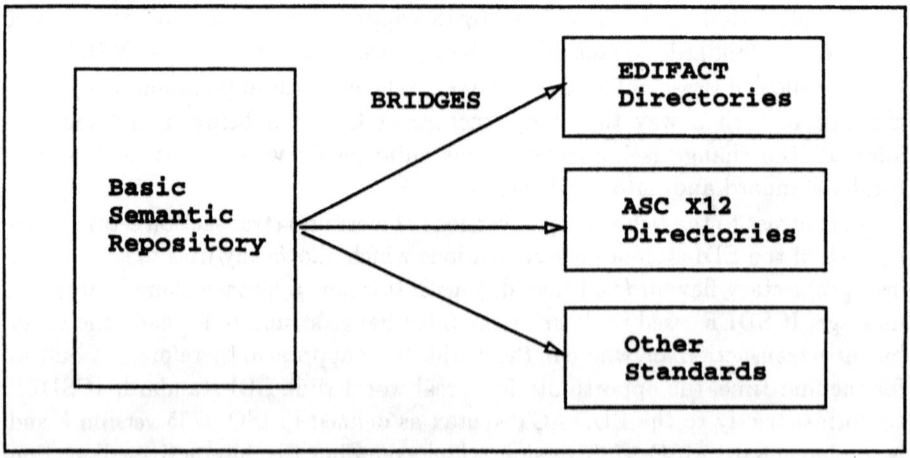

Figure 3.3 BSR to EDI Directory Bridge

first without being hampered by the standardisation process and avoiding high cost overheads are important goals to achieve.

These goals can only be achieved by automating the standardisation process. As the process is one involved in implementing EDI it would seem logical to apply EDI technology to the standardisation process for the BSR. The principles of an automated standardisation process for the Basic Semantic Repository utilising EDI technology (figure 4) is as follows:

1. Each EDI Server has its local BSR. This can be either a full BSR or restricted to specific business scenarios; it can be maintained automatically from the National BSR or the software producers BSR. This decision will be made by the system implementer in conjunction the software producer.

2. Each application programmer has a full BSR which is maintained in line with a National BSR, using EDI technology, by calling the National BSR and requesting an alignment transaction on a regular basis.

3. There is one International BSR which is maintained by and maintains each of the National BSRs using EDI technology using alignment transactions as for the local BSRs.

4. When a system designer or application programmer builds the ICSDEF for a new business application program, the software producer's BSR is searched for the correct label for each data element to be included. If the data element is not found in the BSR, and the software producer's

BSR is verified as being right up to date with the National BSR, then the programmer defines the new data element and adds it to the software producer's BSR being used. This sets in train a whole chain of automated procedures to achieve a world-wide standardisation of the new data element that has been defined.

An important difference between this new proposed method of standardisation of EDI and the old concept is that with this new concept, whenever a new data element is needed, it is added to the BSR immediately and implemented forthwith without waiting for the standardisation procedure to approve it.

By contrast, the current EDI standards approach is to insist business be put on hold until the lengthy standards process accepts it. Presumably, if a change to the standard is not approved, business is supposed stay on hold indefinitely.

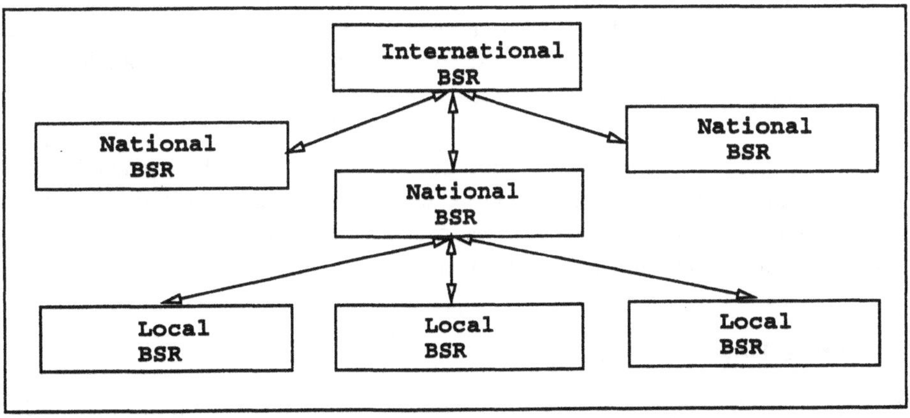

Figure 3.4 Automatic BSR Standardization

Adding new Data Elements

A set of very tight rules is devised for determining the label to be applied to a data element. These rules must ensure, as closely as possible, that if independent persons were to describe the same data element, the same label would be determined. Obviously, prior to devising these rules and proving them over some time in the field, it would have to be assumed that some variation in determining labels will occur and a monitoring system for duplicates included in the process.

The steps in the proposed EDI-based automated standardisation procedures are as follows:

1. Whenever a data element is added to a software-producer's BSR, that BSR maintenance system automatically sends the transaction to the National BSR server, where it is added. A bridge key which identifies the exact location of the element in the National BSR is returned to the originating BSR. All local BSRs receive the new data element when they next call in to the National BSR for alignment.

2. The National BSR administrator (a Business Information Systems expert) checks each new entry. If the new element duplicates an existing data element, the administrator tags that element with the bridge key of the element it duplicates. This is conveyed back to the originating BSR and to any other BSRs that have received the new data element.

3. On finalisation of the new data element by the National System Administrator, the National BSR server automatically forwards the new data element onto the National BSR, where the identical procedure takes place as at the National level. Bridge keys are returned to the National BSR from which they are distributed to the local BSRs as they call into the National BSR server for alignment.

In this way, new Electronic Commerce transactions can be designed, built and implemented without being hindered or delayed by the standardisation process. The standardisation process becomes a servant to assist business to use Electronic Commerce, not an end in itself.

Changing Data Elements

A change is processed as a new data element and processed through the BSR standardisation process as before. The transaction carries the bridge key of the data element which it supersedes. If the change is descriptive only and is approved at both the National and International levels as not affecting the usage of the existing data element, the change, identified by the bridge key of the original data element is returned and distributed via the alignment transactions. If the change would alter the use of the original data element, it is returned as a new data element.

3.5 Removing The Inhibitions

In this section, the solutions offered by flexible messaging are compared against the problems encountered by EDI users that were reported in section 2 to examine its effectiveness toward improving the practicality of the use of EDI technology for Electronic Commerce. There is only ever the need for one standard - ICSDEF. So this, for the first time brings the capability of true standardisation to EDI technology.

3.5.1 EDI-Enabling Of Application Programs

Figure 5 shows the generic structure of an application program used for both interactive input from a screen and EDI input in 3NF. The conversion procedure might be as follows:

- Eliminate the screen handling.
- Eliminate the form assembly.
- Replace the conversion to 3NF to read in the data in 3NF.
- Re-orient the integrity checks from the screen handler to the 3NF records (ie change the data element label in the integrity checking logic).

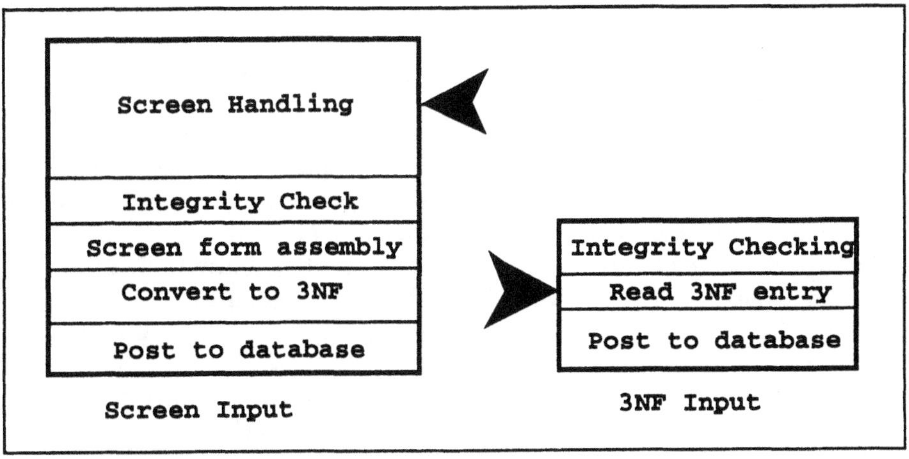

Figure 3.5 EDI-enabling Applications

By actually doing this on a real purchasing program and a real customer order entry program, the total conversion time (in MS BASIC) was 4 hours of relatively easy work. Converting the same programs to work from a flat file produced by the EDI-EDGE translator was 58 hours, but involved quite a lot of learning and was not so easy. The software producers working party felt their experience would be similar.

From this experiment, it is concluded that the flexible messaging approach goes a long way to solve the edi-enablement problem inhibiting the wide-spread adoption of EDI technology for Electronic Commerce.

3.5.2 Implementation

The endless meetings by each industry group working party to reach a consensus as to which version of each message will be used by that industry group and then how it will be implemented have both been eliminated by flexible messaging. The objectives that the working parties now need to discuss and agree is the level of functionality of the application programs they are using.

Now the focus of the users is correctly centred on the business side of Electronic Commerce and EDI has been returned to the areas of expertise needed to handle it - the application programmers and the EDI Server and made transparent to the users.

Translators have been replaced by the EDI Server. The big difference between the two software systems is that translators are mapped by hand whereas the mapping process in the EDI Server is fully automated making changes totally automatic. This means that when the initiating application is changed (which changes the structure of the data interchange), the responding trading partner has to be advised of the change and remember to have the responding translator modified at precisely the right moment to avoid problems in the operation of the business transaction, whereas with the EDI Server, the initiating EDI Server takes care of the whole process automatically without the responder even needing to know it happened.

The standardisation process is no longer totally absorbed in the structure of the message; this is now automated and invisible to the users. Now the concentration is on the business issues and the application programs (currently totally ignored) that actually process the transaction.

The interchange of data structured to 3NF and the ability to link the EDI Server into the same module with the application program enables a one-step operation from the network to the application program. This makes it much easier for small to medium businesses to take advantage of EDI by eliminating the cost of translators, reducing the complication of operating the software and reducing the cost to the system vendor of operating the help desk.

Moving away from the fixed segment structure of current standardisation methods to flexible segment structures results in a major reduction in the amount of overhead in the interchange structure. The construction of messages under current standards methods requires that the structure of a segment that is already defined cannot be changed and rather than place in a new segment a data element that already exists in another segment, that other segment should be included in the message. The result is that the number of characters used in the segment tag and the delimiters marking the position of unused data elements in the segment often exceeds the number of characters of actual data.

3.6 An Easy Way Forward

The remaining problem is how to convert from the current EDI standardisation methods to flexible messaging. One can hardly expect the whole world to reprogram and then stop work at a particular instant to change over.

Typically, flexible messaging has a simple answer to this problem as well. The ICSDEF message is used to describe the structure of the data being interchanged. It can therefore be used to describe any variety of current "standard" messages or transaction sets as well as the new 3NF flexible messages.

A computer program has been written to build a database from an EDIFACT directory. Another program is then able to extract the ICSDEF for any specific message, set of messages or the whole directory. An ICSDEF is now available for every message in four of the EDIFACT directories. To produce a complete set of ICSDEFs from a database extracted from another version of an EDIFACT directory takes approximately 5 minutes, so as each new version of EDIFACT messages are released, it is a trivial matter to produce a new set of ICSDEFs. The ICSDEFs would be held by the local standards authority. In the Australia, this is Electronic Commerce Australia (was EDICA).

Because this solution to the implementation problem is so simple, any EDI user can make a decision to move forward unilaterally - the move does not affect any of the trading partners. The trading partners can stay as they are or move forward at any time.

The procedure for moving from the current fixed message standards to the new flexible message standard is as follows:

1. Obtain a copy of ICSDEF for each version of each "standard" currently in use by each trading partner. This is already known - it is negotiated in the trading partner agreement prior to commencing Electronic trading and was used to set up the translators.

2. Install the EDI Server and the appropriate communications software.

3. Install the ICSDEFs in your EDI directory according to the procedures for the brand of EDI Server being used and specify which ICSDEF is used by which trading partner.

4. Install the ICSDEF to describe the application program's input/output structure.

5. Continue trading, now with the new flexible message facility while retaining the capability to use fixed message standards.

3.7 Conclusions and Recommendations

The technical benefits offered by flexible messaging are:

1. Flexible segment construction means a big reduction in the amount of data that needs to be interchanged.

2. Application programming and program conversion is very much simpler.

The benefits to the software producers are:

1. EDI-enabling of application programs is now much faster and less expensive. This makes it much easier for software producers to enter the Electron Commerce market with EDI-enabled software packages.

2. One-step processing enables EDI-software packages to be shrink-wrapped and reduces help desk support costs though simpler operation procedures for the user.

The benefits to the EDI users are:

1. Flexible messaging maintains 100current standards and enables an easy, unilateral decision by a user to move forward in the use of Electronic Commerce.

2. New application functionality can be introduced without delay and without an expensive and time-consuming effort negotiating the current bureaucratic standardisation processes.

3. Working party effort to operate EDI is reduced considerably and the focus moves from the interchange structure (which is now totally invisible to the user) and move to consideration of purely business issues such as the functionality needed in application programs.

4. One-step operation means operating procedures for Electronic Commerce transactions employing EDI are very much simpler and therefore easier for staff to handle reliably and the costs and delays of handling operation problems reduced.

5. Because software producers are able to convert their packages and write new packages for Electronic Commerce using EDI, a greater selection will appear on the market. This will increase competition between the software producers for the market and result in a wider range of better, more functional, more user friendly and lower cost packages.

6. Business can now react to change must faster and more easily.

3.8 Acknowledgments

My appreciation is expressed to Denis Hill of the ISO, Geneva for discussions and the supply of documentation regarding the ISO/ECE initiative on the BSR and also to Klaus-Dieter Naujok of Premenos for discussions re the ISO/ECE BSR project.

Chapter 4

Machine-Negotiated, Ontology-Based EDI (Electronic Data Interchange)

Fritz Lehmann[1]

4.1 EDI "Old" and "New"

"EDI" (Electronic Data Interchange) is a misnomer. It's really about automated electronic commercial transactions — the nuts and bolts of electronic commerce — rather than the general electronic interchange of data. EDI has been adopted rather slowly over the past decade; it is reportedly used (at least in some limited form) by 50,000 to 70,000 businesses worldwide, most of them large. It is being used and promoted by some U. S. Government agencies, notably in the Department of Defense.

Prior EDI has been a straightforward electronic version of paper business forms. The classic example is the electronic Purchase Order. There are two main published standards for EDI, namely **EDIFACT**, a United Nations standard used internationally, and **ANSI X12**, a private voluntary standard which predominates in the United States.[32, 3] These are massive compilations of business forms from several industries (shipping, trucking, banking, health care, and others) which have been rearranged by the standards committees into somewhat unified formats.[2]

EDIFACT and X12 are primarily data format standards (although they also specify some other aspects of business transactions). Detailed structural descriptions of electronic formats emulate the structures of business forms. An ordinary paper Purchase Order form is divided into sections on the Seller, Buyer, Product, Price, Tax and Shipping-mode; these in turn are divided into addresses, various codes, quantities, etc.; these are further divided into data fields like Name, Street, City, Code-number, Date, etc. Similarly, an EDIFACT form is a **Message**, which is divided into **Segment Groups** of **Segments**, each consisting of **Data Elements**. For example, form **ORDERS** is a Purchase Order

[1] *GRANDAI* Software, 4282 Sandburg Way, Irvine, CA 92715, and Center for Optimization and Semantic Control, Washington University, Saint Louis, MO 63130, USA, email: fritz@rodin.wustl.edu

[2] The X12 standard is supposed to be phased out in favor of EDIFACT in the next few years, but there are some American EDI users and "camp-followers" (such as X12 consultants and software suppliers) who are fighting the change to EDIFACT.[50]

Message; it has a Segment Group, "**6**: tax-related information", which has a Segment **MOA** for "monetary amount", which is defined using Data Element **6343**, "Currency qualifier", which is a three character code for the role of the currency, such as **007**, "Target Currency" which the standard describes as "The name or symbol of the monetary unit to be converted into."[32]

Although the Messages are defined as sequences of Segments which are defined as sequences of Data Elements, the Data Elements themselves have no formal definitions – they (sometimes) have terse English descriptions, often only a word or phrase (many with "self-explanatory" appended). There is nothing resembling formal semantics or machine-usable information in X12 nor in EDIFACT. EDI elements are "formally defined" only in the sense of data structures, as in "3 alphanumeric characters", without formally defined semantic content.

EDI is now viewed two ways. On the one hand, it is being promoted to its user community of businesses and agencies as the latest in modernity, a vital part of the new "information superhighway". Among EDI specialists and theorists, however, it is recognized that the existing EDI practice is fundamentally flawed and obsolescent. The problems are the fixed form of a standard transaction, and the fact that human beings are required to translate all local data formats (used in application programs and databases) to and from that fixed EDI standard form. In fact it has been reported that over 70% of all EDI actually takes place by emailed or FAXed EDI forms which are both written and read by human beings, with computers having no role in the transaction other than in transmission.[74] This so-called "E"DI is nothing more than human exchange of business forms — widely mocked as the "rip and read environment."[22] Also, the huge X12 and EDIFACT standards themselves do not contain nearly enough information to do EDI: you also have to master your industry-specific "implementation guidelines" in addition to your particular trading-partner-specific "implementation conventions" that spell out just what EDI parts will be used. This requires considerable customized negotiations with each trading partner in advance of any actual EDI business transactions. Dissatisfaction with this current standards-based EDI practice has led to the notion of "**new-EDI**" in which new approaches to flexibility, negotiated transaction forms, and genuine automation of transactions are supposed to transcend the "**old-EDI**" use of X12 and EDIFACT. In particular, it is intended that EDI reflect the diversity and flexibility of modern business practice, while freeing potential smaller users from having to hire specialists to master complicated data format standards. It is also intended that transactions between businesses will be integrated with reports and forms used within a business (or enterprise); EDI should be tied into commercial business communication products like Lotus Notes. There is an email list "edi-new" dealing with these and related issues. (To subscribe, as of 1995, send a message to `edi-new-request@tegsun.harvard.edu`.)

4.2 Real-World Semantics for EDI

In current EDI practice, human beings in two different organizations must negotiate to agree in advance on the specific protocols for Purchase Orders, etc. Programmers then create translators from the local database format of the source into standard EDI format, and from EDI to the local database format of the target system. The two communicating computer systems do not "know" what is in the segments and fields – they can only check for syntactic correctness at best. The only *meaning* is in English language remarks and definitions in the standards documents, and in the fact that human beings are checking the printed versions of the transactions. In future EDI and Electronic Commerce, each system will have a conceptual definition of what it *means* to be, say, a "confirmation", and it will be able to detect automatically whether a confirmation in a particular transaction makes any sense. The basic terms in any such definition will come from deep "**ontologies**" for primitive subjects like time, space, human activity, enterprise models, etc.

An **ontology** in the recent AI and database sense is an elaborate conceptual schema of generic domain concepts and relations (often in the form of a **semantic network**[40, 70]) with constraints or axioms, and with a formal **lexicon** or **concept-dictionary**; in a semantic network-based system, the definitions themselves are further networks. Of course at some point you have to have some undefined "semantic primitives" – the object is to have relatively few of these. An ontology is *not* a data definition or metadata schema — rather it is a system of *generally useful, real-world* concepts, relations and constraints in the domain of interest. The definitions are not just structural; they also specify the meaning of the elements of the structure in real-world terms. (So the computer systems will be "aware" that no person is a diagram, that no zip code is a tax, that an American city is geographically within a state, etc.)[3]

Is this "new-EDI" or "old-EDI"? Theoretical complaints about EDIFACT and X12 are varied, but to analyze them you can divide the EDIFACT and X12 standards into two aspects: form and content. Most of the protests against EDIFACT and X12 are against allegedly outdated and inflexible (and often confusing) prescriptions for arrangement and encoding of data — matters of form. The real value in EDIFACT and X12, however, is in their content: their abstract *conceptualization* of the world of commerce into a rich categorical system of times, places, persons, vehicles, containers, measurements, transactions, etc. Although it is still specified only informally (often merely hinted at), this concept system is the product not only of years of standardization, but of more than a century of pragmatic thought about forms and the information needed for business transactions. EDI categories are most of the generic commercially useful categories in *our world*.

[3] This is the hardest point to convey to many people steeped in database work, programming and information systems analysis. An ontology is not about data at all (unless it happens to be an ontology of information structures). A CITY is not a string! Defining CITY does not mean deciding about alphanumeric characters — it involves people, places, residences, spatial proximity, government, etc.

Two recent, related EDI intiatives will be mentioned below: the **BSR** (Basic Semantic Repository) is relevant to the "ontology-based" part of this chapter, whereas Ken Steel's "new-EDI" **ICSDEF** proposal for EDIFACT is more relevant to the "machine-negotiated" part.

The practical *cost* of the ontology-based approach is the large amount of careful work needed to develop the deep ontologies and to translate known standard data elements into them, with lengthy conceptual definitions. Picture a lawyer specifying what is and is not a "container" in great detail, as opposed the the comparatively trivial effort of listing some common container words in the X12 Data Element 211. The specification will include such facts as:

> *"If Thing A is in Container B, and B is shipped in Vessel C, then A is shipped in Vessel C."*

which are obvious to people but initially unknown to computers. Fortunately most of this rather difficult work needs to be done only once, since the real-world concepts in the base-ontologies used for EDI will change only very gradually if at all once they are defined. (The TIME ontology is an example.)

The practical *benefits* are many. First, computers will be able to take over most of the expensive "by hand" reasoning now required to map one data system to an EDI standard or to another data system, and the computer will be able to deduce (and exploit) many things now known only to a human being. If conceptual definitions have been provided for the files and fields in the local databases, the computer can determine what the appropriate standard EDI structure and elements are, automatically. No longer will the business user have to ponder, "Gee, is my weekend delivery a matter of dates or of time-periods?" Also, entirely new trade objects can be created and in a sense "understood" by the participating computer systems, e.g. a standard *40-foot ship container* could be modified to create the new concept *35-foot refrigerated ship container* and the computers would know that it has less storage capacity, is colder, that more of them fit in an area, etc. In addition, the computer can automatically reconcile different measurement systems, time-period capabilities, container capacities etc. Further savings on database maintenance are possible due to the ability to dynamically change the meaning of identifiers, needed due to changes in organizations, manufacturing processes, nomenclature, encodings, or other "domain evolution." [81]

Another benefit is that the kind of conceptual analysis required to create formal definitions is exactly what is needed anyway to bring some order to the redundant, inconsistent and confused X12 and EDIFACT standards as they now exist. When the practical-minded businessmen who created X12 and EDIFACT got together, they combined fields from all kinds of business forms very haphazardly; there was no consistent intellectual guidance to detect redundancy or resolve inconsistency. Currently the standards are getting bigger and bigger; whether they are getting much better is debatable.

4.3 EDI as Integration

The EDI challenge is really a special case of the general database integration or enterprise integration challenge:

> **One system, set up in a certain way for certain purposes, has to communicate information to another system, set up a different way with different data-names and structures (and maybe for different purposes), but with subject-matter common to both systems.**

The main distinction of EDI is that EDI transactions create real, enforceable legal obligations between separate parties.

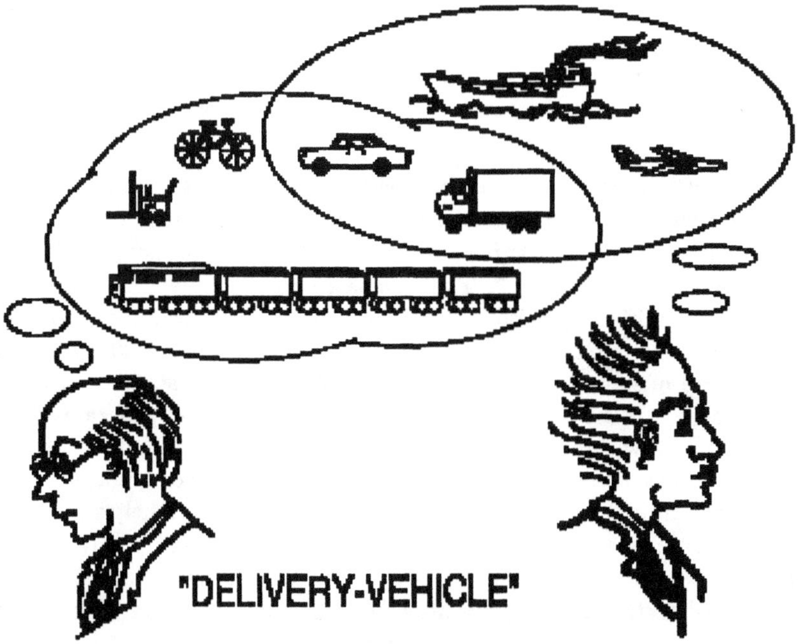

Figure 4.1: The designers of two business-partners' application programs had different ideas of what a 'DELIVERY-VEHICLE' is.

The need for ontology-based integration (of all heterogeneous data systems, including EDI) is based on looking at where the money is spent. It is generally estimatted that 80% of corporate and government software costs go towards "maintenance". The bulk of "maintenance" involves translating data formats from one system to an incompatible system (updating a legacy system or getting two or more different systems to share data). This is a multi-billion dollar expense annually. Some sophisticated schema-integration tools have been created, notably by Navathe and Elmasri and their colleagues[52], and there has been theoretical work by Geller, De Michiel and others on using the pure structure of records to assist in mapping data from one system to another.[26, 21] But everybody comes up against the fact that he or she can't trust the field-names and record-names, and the fact that records about the same subject-matter are differently arranged by different designers. This is the "Semantic Wall". Formal tools can only help so much. The real obstacle is that the computer has no idea (criterion on which it can act) of what the data is *about*. A human being has to read the documentation and address questions like: "Does 'DELIVERY-VEHICLE' for system A include aircraft, as in system B, and if not, how can we use B's database of deivery-vehicles for the 'DELIVERY-VEHICLE' records needed by A?" The designers of the systems may have had different but overlapping intended meanings of 'DELIVERY-VEHICLE'; see Figure 4.1. As long as the documentation (if any!) is in natural language, the meanings are unavailable to the computer. If the meaning of a field or record, in a shared real-world ontology, is provided for two systems in a formal language, the translation can be automatic — except for those borderline instances which require real human judgement. Without this, all translations, tedious and routine though they be, have to be done by hand at great expense by programmers and systems analysts. This is a whole industry.

In EDI you have the same problem. Either you translate by hand from your local data structures to and from an EDI standard directly, or you use a commercial tool that helps you structure some records (flat files) to match EDI formats in the first place. See Figure 4.2. These tools are the **"EDI translators"** which are the most prominently marketed EDI software. They are almost entirely syntactic (not semantic) parsers and translators, stripping off the "EDI envelope" and getting rid of some of the (peculiar) formatting in the standard EDIFACT or X12 messages. But this doesn't make the problem go away, because the rest of your enterprise will not be conceptually aligned to the EDI standard, so the painstaking translation of data formats must now take place again, but between files within the enterprise. See part B of Figure 4.2. Even with helpful translation aids, like graphic "mappers," human analysis, hand-translation and integration is still required. This is the big money drain. EDI consultants estimate that the effort of correctly mapping this already-"translated" EDI data format to the user's application system costs over fifteen to twenty times the EDI translator software costs, even for routine business using a tiny subset of all the possible EDI messages.

It has been suggested that an entire business enterprise could have all its application programs conform semantically to the current EDI standard messages and data elements from the start, thus avoiding semantic translation and hand integration. Although some accounting application programs may advertise themselves as "EDI enabled" in future, the fact is that no major enterprise is going to subordinate its business goals and information-processing methods to the antiquated and haphazardly documented current EDI standards.

Among other reasons for using a formal ontology is so that other kinds of systems within an enterprise can communicate intelligently with the EDI pro-

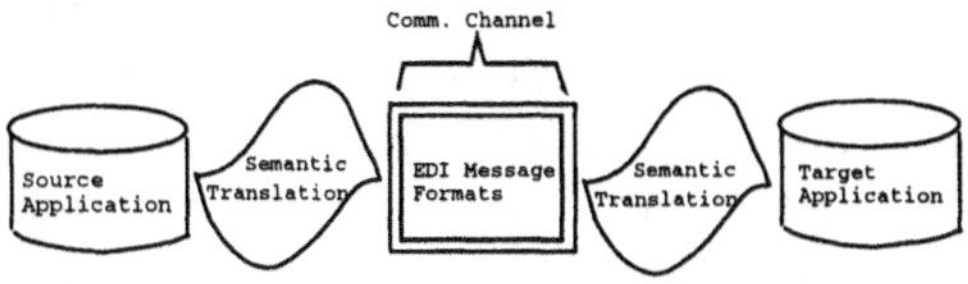

A: Tranditional EDI with custom-programmed translation (hard work) at both ends.

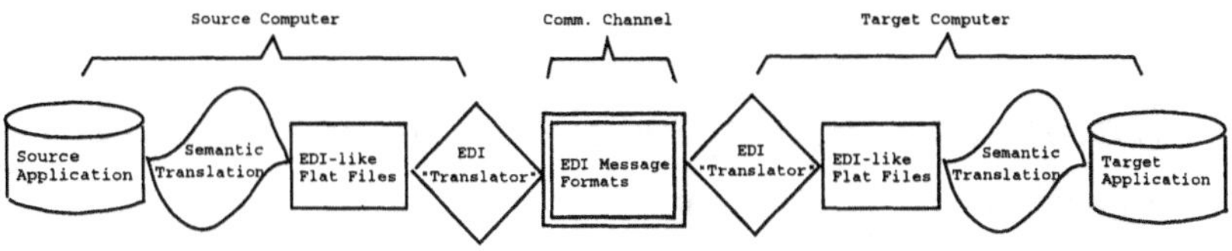

B: Current EDI with "Translator" software at both ends; still requires hard work at both ends.

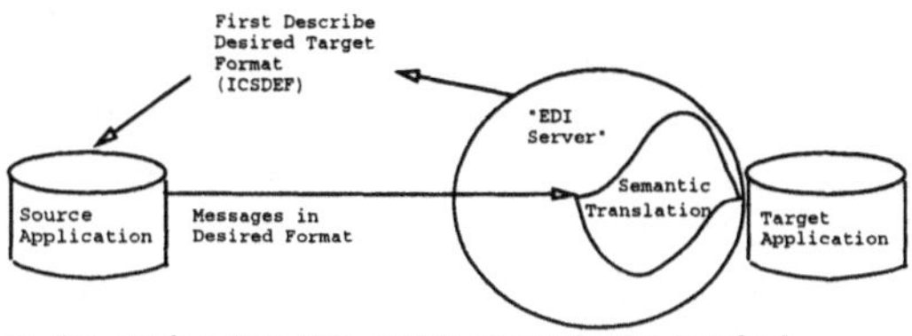

C: Ken Steel's "New EDI" ICSDEF proposal. EDI standard formats are avoided; hard work is only at one end.

Figure 4.2: Theres's no avoiding the semantic translation. A: Direct hand-translation from application formats to EDI(EDIFACT or X12) formats. B: Commercial translators add and remove excess EDI baggage, but the semantic translation to the application program form must still be done by hand. C: Ken Steel's proposed ICSDEF approach gets rid of some needless transformations, but one semantic translation from source form to target form is still needed.

gram. This includes Management Information, CAD systems, accounting systems, manufacturing, etc. For example, the same "widget" ordered by the Army could appear first in the EDI RFQ transaction, then in the Quote and Purchase Order, then in the CAD design system, then in a Numerical Control program for machining, then in a CIM shop-floor program, then in Inventory, then in Accounting, then in a Shipping router, then in a final EDI confirmation, then in the Army's logistics system, etc. The same entity, the widget, has a different (and incompatible) representation in each program now, so intercommunication is nearly impossible. These programs do have different purposes and need different information, but they can be integrated at the knowledge level, and EDI should fit in to this integration scheme. This is a general example of current "enterprise integration" theory.[58] Ontology-based integration is the basis of the CARNOT project, which uses the CYC ontology[31], and of the Summary Schemas Model (SSM), which uses *Roget's Thesaurus*.[10]

4.4 Relevant Ontologies for Product Description, Medicine and Law

At present the EDI standards have a notion of the price paid for a product, but no notion of what that product is, nor its proper specification parameters. There is just a human-readable description, an arbitrary designated part-number, or something similar. This limitation is becoming obsolescent. The **PDES/STEP standards** (Standard for the Exchange of Product Model Data) for manufactured products are now beginning to emerge (complicated standards for detailed product descriptions and specifications; they now cover machined shapes, CAD specifications, assemblies, electronic components and some other areas).[16] These will eventually be extended to other areas of commerce. STEP contains a quasi-ontology which should be grounded in lower-level formal ontologies of space, geometric regions, measurement, etc. A PDES/STEP product description in a Request For Quotes could automatically trigger EDI quotes from capable manufacturers, subcontractors or suppliers, based on the fact that their products are formally subsumed by the description of the desired product in the RFQ. PDES/STEP's language **Express** is now being linked into the "knowledge level" and defined conceptually. Coupled to EDI and STEP, a computer will "understand" automatically that a Purchase Order to ship four Mack Trucks in one Post Office Mailsack is ill-advised.

Similarly, the medical EDI establishment can tie its work into the extensive conceptual standardization taking place at the National Library of Medicine.[47] If a particular general medical syndrome is authorized for insurance reimbursement, the taxonomies and semantic networks in the **UMLS** could be exploited to help determine if more specific disease reports in a transaction fall within the reimbursable general category. There are similar concept systems for treatments, procedures, and medication. The medical insurance industry already has a very large catalogue of reimbursable conditions; this catalogue could be integrated with UMLS and ontological EDI.

Even the area of legal regulations is being studied and formalized at the conceptual level for computers, although this work is still at the early research stage. If and when such systems become practical, logical formulations of the original regulatory language can be used as a formal constraint on EDI transactions. Based on conceptual rules and definitions, U.S. Government procurement could have built-in machine safeguards against certain unsound, nonsensical or illegal transactions. A certain RFQ could trigger: "Sorry, this violates the regulation on minority participation in Regulation CFR XXX:xxx;x(x)iiiv because ..." The fact that EDI transactions have the effect of changing ownership and generating legal obligations means that much of the semantics will ultimately depend on applicable commercial law.

Various standards, thesauri and industry-wide data dictionaries should be mapped automatically to corresponding EDI concepts once the data elements have been given conceptual definitions. The American Petroleum Institute's massive **Petroleum Data Dictionary,** for example, has yet to be mapped to the PIDX petroleum-related subset of the X12 EDI standard, even though both were created by the same organization (API) and deal with overlapping subject-matter. All "document"-related data elements and codes should be coordinated with the increasingly important **Z39.50 standard** for information retrieval, first developed by libraries and used now as the basis of GILS (the Government Information Locator Service). In Z39.50, the semantics of data elements are specified in special "attribute sets" for bibliographic data, scientific data, etc.

4.5 Negotiated Ontologies and Transactions

EDI would consist of two phases: first a negotiated exchange of ontologies and data-type-definitions to get both partners in synch, then interchange of transaction data.

The new EDI approach will not necessarily prescribe the form of the actual commercial transactions, rather it will prescribe the means by which two computer systems will reach an agreement on common terms and concepts, and on the particular set of data needed for a transaction. We assume that systems will share at least some very basic generic ontologies (for their most primitive terms) even if they have very different needs and capabilities. The negotiation consists of:

A. Identify Parties - establish the identities and authorities of the parties (the KQML language, with extensions, may be useful for this); assert legal power to undertake transactions (with cryptographic and/or cybernotary authentication if neccessary)

B. Prior Accord - refer to common ontologies, definitions and forms established in previous dealings, if any

C. Common Grounding - identify a set of common low-level generic ontologies available to both systems, and any standard electronic commerce ontologies which may happen to be common to both parties

D. Term Definitions - a statement by each party of the relevant specialized concepts normally used in a transaction, defined explicitly using the primitives from the common ontologies

E. Assess Mappings - an assessment of the best possible mappings from the just-defined relevant concepts in each system to those in the other system (the EGG/YOLK reliability hierarchy may be used.[42]).

F. Reconcile Differences - where some relevant concepts fail to map acceptably, explore workarounds and back-up positions; low priority items may be abandoned or defaults assumed

G. Agree on Transactions - mutual descriptions of the desired transactions, or reference to an EDIFACT or X12 transaction codes

H. Agree on Data Required - definition of the data needed for a transaction, omitting superfluous information not demanded by the parties (similar to the proposed ICSDEF message)

I. Agree on Formats - formulate the form to be used: order, field-names, groupings, formats (these are a totally separate matter from the content)

J. Agree on Channels - agree on a particular communications channel, protocols, etc.

K. Agree on Liability - explicitly state the legal liabilities of the parties to perform under the EDI offer, or contract governing this transaction series. State monetary limits of liability, and invoke any guarantors or Letters of Credit.

From this point on, transactions are instances of the agreed-upon form, sent by a party via the agreed-upon channel, unless and until the agreement is revised. A fanciful possible example of this sequence, with all of these parts, appears at the end of this chapter.

The desired flexibility comes from the "negotiated ontology" aspect (items B through F above). Consider: a well-established trading partner presents a newcomer with a proposed ontological agreement (all by machine) which defines the concept of *packing units* with the list of "containers" as used in X12 Element 211; the newcomer can respond by saying "No, for me any containing thing can be a packaging unit, not just the X12 list in Element 211. I send liquids in sealed pipes, which are in fact containers." The responding system is declaring an exception to the previously agreed-upon rule. As long as there is some common ontological ground (common primitives), every transaction set between any two partners can have *negotiated ontological definitions*. This would also interact with the "business rules" of each partner, which could be expressed in terms of the ontology. An example of a business rule would be: "All international transactions over US$1,000.00 must have an encrypted authorization code." Entirely new terms, tokens or "tags" can also be defined "on the fly" conceptually to adjust to specialized business needs. A tag then will really mean exactly what you say it means. A problem with this is that a user would need to understand the intended use at a deep level and be able to express the conceptual definition correctly — a skill not likely to be very universal.

Negotiation of the ontology itself goes beyond the otherwise *avant-garde* idea of using common ontology to integrate disparate databases or enterprises. Here we are integrating the ontologies themselves.[4]

The use of "generic" or universal ontologies may allow novel intersector transactions (i.e. between different industries) to be developed automatically. Concepts of automobile distribution may not be known to a currency trading system, and vice-versa, but if the two need to communicate it should be possible for them to exchange sequences of long and painstaking definitions (based on generic ontology) until a valid transaction between them becomes feasible. Nothing in the "new EDI" approach will be fundamentally incompatible with the existing EDIFACT or X12 standards. On the contrary, an ontology-based EDI would provide deep semantics for the Data Elements of the existing standards.

4.6 The Formal Description Language

The semantic definition of the meaning of an EDI element can be expressed in a **semantic network**[40, 70], a **frame system** or a standard **logic** format. The main thing lacking in basic *frames* is the proper handling of *negation* and *disjunction*. These are handled correctly in **Conceptual Graphs**, John F. Sowa's order-sorted (i.e. with a type hierarchy) semantic network system with negated "contexts"[69], and in the ARPA Knowledge Sharing Effort's **KIF** (Knowledge Interchange Format) language (together with Tom Gruber's **Ontolingua** frame language)[27]. Most of these languages were first developed in the area of Artificial Intelligence. The standard form of Conceptual Graphs has (at least) the full expressive power of typed Predicate Logic, as does KIF. So you could define for EDIFACT:

> *"A Purchase Order of type-X is one without terms of delivery (segment group 11) if it has either fixed transport means (segment group 9) or if the delivery schedules are specified (segment group 15)."*

[4] The science-fiction movie *Colossus: the Forbin Factor* has an exchange of ever-more-sophisticated mathematical concepts between two supercomputers starting from 1+1=2. Daniel Defoe's *Robinson Crusoe* has an initial exchange of concepts between Crusoe and Friday who speak different languages. Some proposals for intial radio communication with intelligent aliens have the same kind of aim. These are extreme versions of ontological negotiation in which the pre-existing common ontological ground (item C above) is presumed to be very minimal. We have to assume the much easier situation in which most concepts relevant to an industry are pretty much agreed-upon.

This requires negation and disjunction. In a graph-based system, a formal conceptual dictionary definition of an element, segment, or transaction-type would specify a **graph-grammar substitution** of a large, descriptive conceptual graph for a small one.

The ISO/IEC JTC1/SC21/WG3/CSMF Interim Rapporteur Group recently met in Seattle to complete the basic **CSMF** or Conceptual Schema Modelling Facility standards proposal (essentially the old IRDS normative language). This includes Conceptual Graphs and the logic language KIF as alternative concept-definition languages.[49] If this CSMF standard moves forward quickly, it should be an appropriate language in which to commence a programme of formal conceptual definitions of EDI objects. KIF itself has been proposed as a separate standard for knowledge interchange (despite some earlier promises to the AI community that it would not be proposed as a standard).

The idea of ontology-based EDI does not imply that all definitions have to be precise. In the EDI world there cannot be a dogmatic definition of precisely what is and is not a "suburb" (X12 Element 309:SB), but we know that Manhattan is not a suburb and that Webster Groves is; we can define some qualities that suburbs certainly should have and other qualities that suburbs certainly should not have – even though this leaves a large "gray area" for human beings to judge the borderline cases. That is, we can state necessary conditions, even though they are not sufficient conditions for classification. There is middle ground between overspecifying everything (so that it is inflexible and obsolescent) and specifying nothing semantically at all as in the current EDI standards. This middle ground can be attained with a system of semantic constraints (rather than precise definitions). Traders can agree completely, for example, that no barge (X12 Element 211:BRG) is a suburb, despite the natural imprecision of both concepts.

4.7 Sources of Ontologies

The main obstacle is not so much finding a suitable logical language; rather it is getting the right underlying "real-world ontology" needed to properly define the business practices involved in EDI. This requires not only sophisticated models of trade and enterprises, but also some of the applicable commercial law, as well as real-world basics such as time, space, events, measurement, people, obligation, etc.

There are several existing base-ontologies being developed now. The **CYC** Project is a well-known example; its common-sense knowledge base is proprietary and secret, although parts of its main ontology are due to be released.[44] Many useful notions appear in the **ARPA Rome Planning Ontology**, a sensible system limited in scope.[23] At Stanford, some ontologies written in KIF and Ontolingua are maintained on line as part of ARPA's Knowledge Sharing Effort and they are freely available. There are a number of proprietary ontologies developed by corporations, such as those of **GE, Oracle, Ontek, Enterprise Integration Technologies, Longman's Publishing** and **Intelligent Text Processing, Inc.** There is also the **Penman/Pangloss Ontology Base**

at USC/ISI[35], the **SNePS Case-Frame Dictionary**[67], and the **CCAT "Conceptual Catalogue"** ontology repository of the PEIRCE Project (a voluntary collaborative worldwide effort to build a testbed for Conceptual Graphs) with which I am associated.[41]

CCAT for example intends to put together a basic core of useful ontologies that can be used for free "off-the-shelf", and it has a special subgroup on **TRADE-ACTIVITIES** which will concern EDI and Electronic Commerce.The current list of intended CCAT ontologies is:

— **Core-ontologies:**
ABSTRACT ALGEBRA & DISCRETE MATH; TIME; SPACE; PART-WHOLE; EVENT/OBJECT/PROCESS; DEEP CASE RELATIONS; REPRESENTATION; MEASUREMENT UNITS; SITUATIONS; CAUSALITY.

— **Non-core subjects:**
GENERAL THESAURI; DIGITAL SYSTEMS; INFORMATION SYSTEMS; COMMUNICATION; ENTERPRISE MODELS; TRADE ACTIVITIES; ADDRESSES; QUASIRATIONAL AGENTS; STORIES/HUMAN ACTIVITIES;EMOTIONS; ONTOLOGY OF NATURAL LANGUAGE; BIBLIOGRAPHY; PHYSICS; QUALITATIVE PHYSICS; MATERIALS; PRODUCT DESCRIPTION; CIM-INDUSTRIAL PROCESSES; SOFTWARE; MEDICINE; LAW.

There are numerous potentially relevant *enterprise models,* like **Carnot, ICAM, CIMOSA, IWI, IBM-CIM, Tove**, and others; these may be used as sources for transaction-related concepts. The concepts underlying ANSI X12 and EDIFACT EDI will be good candidate target-concepts to test the usefulness of these basic ontologies in formal definitions of real-world activity. Another good candidate for target-concepts is the PDES/STEP standard for product descriptions.[16] (STEP and EDI are complimentary, or at least they should be.) Farther afield, I have identified over 150 potentially relevant concept-systems including commercial, academic and historical sources. *Roget's Thesaurus* is the ontological basis for semantic data integration in the SSM (Summary Schemas Model) project.[10]

Commerce develops and changes dynamically. As the real world of business changes, the TRADE ACTIVITIES ontology will change substantively. Underlying core ontologies like TIME and SPACE will probably need some ongoing refinement although major disruptions should be rare. We would need to update "ontology-based EDI" just as we now have to update X12 and EDIFACT (except that it would be more work, and maybe more interesting work). The benefit would be that once the ontology is updated, machines all over the world would be able to respond automatically to the changed formats without the current horrendous integration and maintenance expenses — a one-time-effort for each update cycle. This is assuming that the updates will be in the form of new definitions and constraints rather than fundamental changes to the semantic primitives.

4.7.1 Relation to ICSDEF and Basic Semantic Repository (BSR)

Establishing ontological "common ground" automatically by machine-negotiation is a further development beyond the proposed "**ICSDEF message**" (Interchange Structure Definition) currently being urged by Ken Steel of the University of Melbourne as the key to "new-EDI".[74] An ICSDEF message specifies in advance which data fields will be needed in an EDI transaction series between two partners, and it can be tailored to the situation and formatted as the parties see fit. In effect it obviates the need to follow the standard formats for transactions in X12 and EDIFACT. There is one translation, from source file to target file, enabled by an ICSDEF "wrapper" that describes the format of the source file; often it will be a flat file. This scheme depends crucially on the ability to annotate the fields in the source format with standard semantic identifiers that can be used by the target system to build its own file from the transmitted information. There is still the whole problem of semantic integration of disparate systems, as shown by the 'semantic translation' squiggle in part C. of Figure 4.2.

Ontology-based EDI also goes well beyond the idea of the **BSR (Basic Semantic Repository)** initiative recently begun by the ISO committee dealing with EDIFACT.[78] The BSR is an important step in the right direction since it is supposed to be a repository of semantic EDI terms with detailed definitions (defined in English), annotated with "*bridges*" from the BSR terms to specific elements of EDIFACT, X12 and any other EDI standards. Unfortunately, the BSR contains no way to define new terms such that the computer has any way of acting on the definition; the BSR definitions and constraints, existing only in natural language, are beyond computer processing for the forseeable future.[5]

The proposed BSR *"definition"* of CITY is "the name of a residential area with defined boundaries." (City blocks, housing subdivisions, retirement homes, wards and census tracts would be undesired examples of this underspecified definition.) An *"additional information"* field says "a city is a generic term comprising city, town, village which only differ in size and legal requirements." It's presumed that you know what city, town and village mean, and it would appear to exclude settlements, kraals, medinas and other terms. Nothing in these English-language fields lets a computer know that people live in cities, that cities have governments, that they occupy geographic space, that a typical village is not bigger than a typical city, etc. In ontology-based EDI the definition would be longer, formalized, and based on primitives from core ontologies about people, places, governments and so on. A *true* "semantic repository" would have some low-level definitions (of primitives) that depend on human interpretation, but most definitions would be composite and the computer could interpret the definition and detect violations of the stated constraints using known inference techniques. In essence the negotating programs would be free to define new

[5] At present the BSR has not been implemented in much detail. Recently the BSR committee has decided to coordinate with the ISO 11179 Meta Data Definitons Committee, which is taking the ontological approach recommended here for defining data elements, although the definitions are not formalized.

terms in a general-purpose formal language with something like the expressive power of natural language.

Defining the semantic concepts in EDIFACT and X12 more precisely is a good first step towards machine-usable definitions. The great value of X12 and EDIFACT is the vast ontology they (implicitly and informally) contain. My focus is basically the same as the BSR project: careful attention to the content. I agree with Ken Steel that all sorts of transaction forms can be usefully negotiated, described, defined, and used, but only *if* there is a semantic basis for translating their content from one system to another.

4.8 Culture Clash

One obstacle to the adoption of this kind of proposal is a very deep "culture clash." The people in the EDI world are very practical-minded business people struggling to master an alien technology which already seems very high-tech to them (despite the fact that from a computer science point of view, EDI methods are about 20 years out-of-date). The most advanced EDI thinkers are those involved in certain Working Groups in the standards committees. Even there, there is still a "business forms" mentality — someone in, say, the barge or trucking industry has always had a place on a form for "return consignment agent" or the like, and he or she won't recognize that this is either conceptually identical to the same idea in another industry, or is superfluous from the start. Academics and philosophically minded theorists are viewed suspiciously ("the propeller-heads," to quote a prominent architect of the X12 EDI standard). It's bad enough to mention computer science at all, but when you start talking about conceptual hierarchies, ontological/philosophical analysis, and Artificial Intelligence, you might as well have stepped in from the Twilight Zone. EDI to many of them is strictly a matter of Wal-Mart demanding electronic Invoices and Purchase Orders. It is doubtful whether the current EDI community could ever be receptive to the approaches described here. The impetus is likely to originate elsewhere, such as in the CommerceNet, EINet and similar communities.

4.9 Conclusions

1. EDI is held back by inflexibility and complexity for users. This is partly due to the antiquated X12 and EDIFACT standards.

2. Truly automatic translation between two disparate databases, or between EDI and a database not set up just for EDI, requires machine representation of the concepts and meaning of the data schema, not just the schema.

3. The database world has reluctantly begun to recognize this, and that common ontologies are needed for true automated integration. The EDI community, due to its particular culture, may never realize it.

4. The real-world "common ontology" is actually the most valuable thing about EDIFACT and X12, but it is informal, in English, and unavailable for any computational use.

5. The current major Artificial Intelligence efforts to build large generic ontologies should be applied to automate EDI translations and do useful inference; also, AI ontologists can exploit thousands of practical real-world concept-categories from EDI standards EDIFACT and X12. These provide good target concepts for us to define.

4.10 Appendix: A Stylized Electronic Conversation

Machine-negotiated, ontology-based EDI is not yet implemented. An informal example will suggest some of the more ambitious long-term goals. The following is a fanciful exchange in stylized English between two automatic trader-programs using some of the features listed above. The actual negotiation would be in a formal language by high-speed link between computers, taking perhaps a second. The point of this example is to illustrate the possibilities of such a negotiation occurring between machines with little or no human intervention; in particular, **no prior human negotiation between trading partners is assumed.** Any early implementation of ontology-based EDI would assume much more compatibility between the parties and would not attempt to resolve all the kinds of elaborate semantic problems shown below. Here, two very different electronic traders **Bran:** and **Chap:** automatically form an agreement governing a future series of transactions:

A. Identify Parties

Bran: `I am BransonExplosives. My DUNS number is 1234567.`
`My encrypted signature key is AAAAAAA.`
`I respond to your Request for Proposals #244 for 100,000 VOTARY CANDLES and 10,000 CANDLE-HOLDERS.`
Chap: `I am USMC-ChaplainCorps-Procurement.`
`My encrypted signature key is BBBBBBBB.`
`I accept that you are BransonExplosives.`

B. Prior Accord

Chap: `Have we dealt before?`
Bran: `Not directly. I sold training warheads to your parent system USMC-LOGISTIC-BARSTOW on 9/9/1996.`
Chap: `USMC-LOGISTIC-BARSTOW just confirmed that to me, I accept it.`
Bran: `Three ontological protocols were agreed upon: generic MONEY, TIME and a customized SAFETY agreement.`
Chap: `I don't have SAFETY; I inherit TIME and MONEY from USMC-LOGISTIC-BARSTOW, which have not changed.`
Bran: `TIME and MONEY have not changed for me either. Let's agree to use our earlier TIME and MONEY ontologies for our transactions.`

Chap: Agreed.

C. Common Grounding

Chap: I have access to the CCAT core ontologies:
SPACE, PART-WHOLE, ABSTRACT-ALGEBRA, EVENT-OBJECT-PROCESS, CAUSALITY, SITUATIONS, REPRESENTATION, MEASUREMENT-UNITS and DEEP-CASE. I have CCAT non-core ontologies GENERAL THESAURI, DIGITAL SYSTEMS, INFORMATION SYSTEMS, GEOMETRY, MATERIALS, HUMAN-ACTIVITY, QUASIRATIONAL-AGENT, ENTERPRISE MODELS, TRADE ACTIVITIES, and ADDRESSES.
I have CYC ontologies TypicalAmerican, CommerceStuff and GovernmentWork. For English words I have Roget-Tagged. I have ...
Bran: I too have access to those CCAT ontologies except for GEOMETRY & MATERIALS. Of the CYC ontologies, I have only CommerceStuff.

D. Term Definitions

Chap: My special PAYMENT-TERMS for procurement are NEXT-QUARTER.
Bran: I have only EDIFACT PAYMENT-TERMS as listed in Element 4279; there is no EDIFACT data code there called ''NEXT-QUARTER''.
Chap: I will define it for you in terms of our shared TIME and MEASUREMENT-UNITS ontologies. See the formal ontological definition of QUARTER (EDIFACT Data Element Value 2151:3M). Any YEAR has FOUR NONOVERLAPPING OFFICIAL TIME-PERIODS of 3 MONTHS each, called QUARTERs, consisting of the JANUARY to MARCH period, the APRIL to JUNE period, ... If an INVOICE is RECEIVED by us on a DATE, one MONTH is ADDED to that DATE; the resulting DATE occurs WITHIN a QUARTER and we PAY the INVOICE in US-MONEY by MAILED CHECK to the SELLER on the LAST DAY of the QUARTER NEXT AFTER that QUARTER.
Bran: Understood and Agreed.

[It's also conceivable that the product itself could be mutually defined in addition to the usual EDI terms:]

Bran: Your Request for Proposals requires 100,000 ''votary candles'' and 10,000 ''candle holders''; I can supply 100,000 ''roman candles'' and 10,000 ''candle holders''. What exactly is a ''votary candle''?
Chap: A ''votary candle'' is a CYLINDRICAL OBJECT with a ''wick'' which is to be LIGHTED and BURNED. Its PURPOSE is BURNING from one END to the other, thereby RADIATING LIGHT to be seen by PERSONS.
Bran: My ''roman candle'' is a CYLINDRICAL OBJECT with a ''fuse'' which is to be LIGHTED and BURNED. Its PURPOSE is BURNING from one END to the other, therby RADIATING LIGHT to be SEEN by PERSONS. Does my ''fuse'' mean your ''wick''?
Chap: A ''wick'' is a PIECE of STRING which is LIGHTED and BURNED at one END so as to LAST a TIME-PERIOD.
Bran: So is a ''fuse''. My ''roman candles'' may comply with your Request for Proposals. What is ''votary''?
Chap: ''Votary'' means something which is BROUGHT to an ALTAR by a PERSON for a religious PURPOSE. A *typical* VOTARY CANDLE is made of BEESWAX, and it BURNS QUIETLY for 12 HOURS to 36 HOURS.
Bran: My roman candles could be brought by a PERSON to an ALTAR. A *typical* ROMAN CANDLE is made of GUNPOWDER and it BURNS LOUDLY in from 1/4

of a SECOND to 3 MINUTES. My ''candle holders'' are METAL and fit within your specified PDES/STEP SHAPE and MATERIALS definition for ''candle holder''.

E. Assess Mappings

Bran: I understand PAYMENT-TERM:NEXT-QUARTER since our definitions are now logically equivalent. This is a perfect mapping. My CANDLE-HOLDERS fully comply with your PDES/STEP specification.
Chap: Yes, agreed.
Bran: OK. Our strict definitions of ''candles'' are logically inequivalent but not inconsistent-- the concepts could overlap.
Chap: I require more than possible overlap for this Request For Proposals. I require an ''EGG/YOLK mapping reliability level 13'' or better for the VOTARY-CANDLES concept.
[in EGG/YOLK reliability theory for data mapping (see [42]), level 13 requires at least an overlap between the typical *instances of both concepts]*
Your *typical* candle BURNS LOUDLY in from 1/4 of a SECOND to 10 MINUTES; my *typical* candle BURNS QUIETLY for 12 HOURS to 36 HOURS. The intersection of these *typical* classes of candles is empty, so the reliability of the class-mapping is less than EGG/YOLK level 13. Apparently I must reject it.

F. Reconcile Differences

Chap: My requirement for agreement on ''candles'' precludes my accepting that your ROMAN-CANDLES are VOTARY-CANDLES because EGG/YOLK reliability level 13 is not achieved.
Bran: Will you accept the risk that my ''candles'' are incompatible with your ''candles'' if I offer them at a deep discount?
Chap: No. I will not accept that ROMAN-CANDLES means VOTARY-CANDLES at any price.

G. Agree on Transactions

Chap: I require from you a PROPOSAL for 10,000 CANDLE-HOLDERS only (no CANDLES); if it is satisfactory then I will send you a binding EDIFACT-style ''ORDERS'' purchase order; you will confirm with EDIFACT form ''ORDRSP''. Then you will ship me the CANDLE-HOLDERS in boxes bar-coded as SHIPMENTS with a MANIFEST message. Then you will send EDIFACT ''ADVANCE-SHIPPING-NOTICE'' and ''INVOICE'' to me for Payment. This will be done for each box of 100 CANDLE-HOLDERS. Payment terms will be NEXT-QUARTER as we agreed.
Bran: Yes, but I want to ship in lots of 1000 instead of lots of 100.
Chap: Agreed.

H. Agree on Data Required

Chap: Does your proposed INVOICE contain the PARTYs, their ADDRESSes, the INVOICE-DATE, some REPRESENTATION of the PRODUCT, a SHIPPER and a PRICE in U.S. DOLLARS?
Bran: All but the SHIPPER.

Chap: Add the SHIPPER to your invoice form and I will accept it.
Bran: Agreed. SHIPPER is defined in the TRADE-ACTIVITIES ontology and in my local database meta-data; I know my SHIPPERs.
Which data do you normally include in your EDIFACT ''ORDERS'' purchase order form?
Chap: All The EDIFACT ''ORDERS'' fields with non-empty values.
Bran: All I need is 0030 (date-time segment), 0120 (party segment), 960-STEP (item description segment, but in STEP terms), 980 (quantity segment), and 1150 (price segment).
Chap: OK I'll skip all the rest.

I. Agree on Formats
Chap: I can send my purchase orders in the usual EDIFACT format.
Bran: Don't bother. Just use a flat file with tagged fields: XXX, YYY, and ZZZ, comma-delimited and in in any order.
As a military agency you use a 24 hour clock.
Convert it to 12 hour for these transactions, 4 numeric characters followed by 1 alpha character: HHMM{A/P}.
Chap: Agreed.

J. Agree on Channels
Chap: I use the XYZ VAN service, or encrypted MIME email.
Bran: Use encrypted MIME email.

K. Agree on Liability
Chap: We will be bound by cyber-UCC-500 Schedule 6 for government buyers. You will be be bound to perform thereunder, and in addition to indemnify us against any and all damage claims by third parties.
Bran: No. We will not indemnify you for ''any and all damage claims'' by third parties; we will only be liable for performance, breach, and actual damages due to negligence in manufacturing, as is already provided by cyber-UCC-500 Schedule 6.
Chap: (Checking perhaps with a person or an expert system) Agreed.
Bran: We have agreed on everything necessary for our negotiated series of binding transactions. Let us commence. My PROPOSAL will follow. ...

Chapter 5

Changes in the Interchange Agreements

Andreas Mitrakas[1]

5.1 Introduction

Electronic Data Interchange (EDI) is an indisputable economic success for businesses which are technologically oriented and have implemented it already. Traders realise the benefits which EDI can bring in for a company if incorporated into its daily transactions and they want to take advantage of it. Meanwhile, new applications have been developed such as open systems and interactive EDI. These applications can make it easier for new entrants to participate in the electronic transactions and can help businesses apply new ways of communication. The implementation of EDI, however, comes at a cost. Additional new applications in trade methods can hide several legal pitfalls. Pointing them out can help users to enjoy fully the advantages of EDI and help its circulation.

There are certain EDI users who react positively to the measurable as well as the less notable advantages of EDI. However important EDI may be for modern businesses, the vast majority of its potential users do not seem to be very enthusiastic. The overall number of users around the globe lags far behind the expectations of the experts. Users hesitate to change their trusted and well tested practices and make a move towards a new means of business communications. In the early days, EDI emerged as a novel way of business communication between large users. The implementation cost was prohibitive for the average small user who would have liked to participate. The globalisation of trade, however, makes it easier for small and medium sized enterprises (SMEs) to participate in commercial transactions at a global level. Additionally, the wide availability of technology has lowered the cost barrier considerably. However, according to a report [71] only 70000 businesses around the world use EDI for their transactions. The number is indeed very discouraging, because it means that EDI has so far failed to penetrate global trade practices. If EDI is to succeed it is quite important that it does not remain confined to a large users "club" but that it becomes a tool which will ultimately facilitate everyday transactions. In Europe in particular, where a large part of the economic activity is owed to the

[1] Centre for Computers and Law, Erasmus University Rotterdam, P.O. Box 1738, 3000 DR Rotterdam, The Netherlands, e-mail: Andreas@RRJ.FRG.EUR.NL

SMEs, the success of EDI is heavily dependent upon their prompt and positive response.

Law is one of the issues which the users consider to be important for EDI. There are several legal problems in relation to EDI which have already attracted the attention of legal experts. Various ways are open to users in order to address the legal issues of EDI and eventually make electronic transactions legally safe. From a legal standpoint an interchange agreement is the most common and successful way to develop stable and secure electronic trade relations among trade partners. An interchange agreement is a contract effected between the trade partners which aims to anticipate as many as possible of the problems which may come up in the future relations of the parties. EDI does not substantially change the essence of trade but indeed it poses new legal challenges to the users. An interchange agreement may take several forms. The users can choose between a formal, informal, model or self drafted agreement. Usually, they all address issues which pose questions with respect to the legal aspects of the implementation of EDI and they propose solutions which aim to facilitate open and flexible trade. Model interchange agreements are quite important in this respect because they are drafted in a balanced and impartial way. However, the reality can be quite disappointing as long as trade partners use an interchange agreement as an instrument to maximise their benefits derived from the introduction of EDI at the expense of their business counterparts.

5.2 The Theory of the "Rightful Regulation"

An interchange agreement like any other contract should be seen as the "rightful regulation" of the relations of the participants in the electronic trade. An interchange agreement is simply a contract, thus the parties that are involved in drafting one, should follow the principles which have been set down in the general theory of contract law. According to W. Schmidt-Rimpler [56] a contract is a mechanism which has the power to control the relations of the contracting parties rightfully. The parties themselves vest the contract with the power to regulate their relations. This power is established upon the principle of contractual freedom and fairness. The free expression of the will of the participants is the only guarantee of fairness they have. A contract has the ability to produce fair results within the limits of the will of the contracting parties. Schmit-Rimpler introduces the concept that the legal solutions that are proposed in a contract must also be socially acceptable. Thus, any contractual arrangement must feature a certain level of fairness. However, the most important element is the expressed free will of the parties. When a contract lacks the freely expressed consent of the contracting parties it cannot serve its purpose. If the aforementioned conditions are not met, a contract cannot fulfil its function as a means for the rightful regulation of matters. Consequently, a contract can be refused acknowledgement in court.

The theory of Schmidt-Rimpler was later expanded by M. Wolf [56]. Wolf considers contractual freedom to be the most important criterion for the integrity and acceptance of a contract. However, a contract cannot be considered fair unless the participants are equal in terms of economic power and reasoned judgement, such as experience for example. In real life these essential elements hardly ever appear together. Wolf observes therefore, that the lack of these elements gives only a facade of fairness. In this case a court may intervene if requested in order to correct the terms of the contract.

In an interchange agreement it is not always certain that the elements of the above mentioned theory are present. Small users in particular are faced, for example, with rigid corporate policies which dictate the introduction of EDI or the interruption of transactions [83]. The theory of Schmidt-Rimpler and Wolf can be applied in the case of very small users who transact electronically with large ones. Electronic transactions usually take place on the basis of ready made agreements, usually drafted by the larger trade partner. Such agreements are not subject to negotiation before the transactions begin. Sometimes interchange agreements, which also contain unclear terms, can make smaller users feel negatively about the implementation of EDI. The deficiencies of the interchange agreements discourage users from fully implementing EDI. Legal solutions proposed so far may fail to serve adequately the interests of the parties involved, as information systems move from point-to-point applications to open systems. There is a concern about the future of EDI among the small and medium sized enterprises (SMEs), whose role is quite important in Europe. If EDI has a strategic role to play in the future of electronic commerce, it should be implemented in a more regulated and systematic way. EDI law has an important dual role to play in this respect. It is just as important to the individual application, as it is to the strategic target of the widespread use of EDI.

Various organisations around the globe have been working on pointing out, modelling and presenting in a systematic and formal way issues which are related to the legal aspects of the interchange of commercial data. Examples are the TEDIS (Trade EDI Systems) of the Commission of the European Communities, the EDIFORUM in the Netherlands and under the same name in Italy, the EDI association in the UK, the American Bar Association in the US, the EDI Council of Canada and the Electronic Commerce Australia. Such organisations exist in other countries as well. With respect to the interchange agreements, each one of these has produced a model interchange agreement after conducting an in depth study of the legal status of EDI in each of the respective countries or trade regions.

This chapter examines the legal drawbacks of the implementation of EDI among trade partners who have a long lasting co-operation. It gives an inventory of problems that the users may encounter when drafting an interchange agreement. It takes into account the perspective of an open communication environment, where trade relationships are more volatile, partially due to the lack of prior negotiations for the regulation of legal problems. There are a number of contract law and competition issues to consider. It also examines the possibility of finding a way, other than interchange agreements, to regulate EDI relations and contain conflicts. Such a way needs to correspond more effectively to the real needs of the users of open systems. Trade partners should be aware of the fact that legal problems may cause alterations to their plan to implement EDI.

5.3 Model Interchange Agreements

The introduction of EDI in modern business practices found national legislations ill-prepared to help its implementation. The problems which arise may lead to disputes that can escalate severely. Clearly, the intention of the parties when they start electronic transactions is not to end up in court. There are a number of core issues which, if the parties can agree upon beforehand, could make it easier for them to reach a solution faster and contain the dispute. Drafting those issues in a single contract can offer a more formalised solution to the parties involved. A model interchange agreement (MIA) is an attempt to address the legal problems of the implementation of EDI in a formal way and to propose solutions. Furthermore, model agreements have an additional advantage for the users because due to the fact that the drafting parties are not directly involved in the particular electronic trade relationship they should be considered to be impartial.

There are other kinds of agreements which are more informal and they are more frequently used. Such agreements are the self-drafted agreements, which are drafted by themselves. In other cases, an interchange agreement may be oral and it is an informal agreement. Such agreements can usually take a very partial view of the regulated issues. It is doubtful if this kind of agreement can keep up with the principle of a contract as a fair and rightful solution as it is represented in the model agreements.

5.3.1 MIA or DIY?

Not every EDI user is able to draft his/her own interchange agreement. Drafting an agreement [48] is a rather expensive and complicated task. The drafting process involves a small team of specialised persons. The minimum requirement would be at least one legal expert and one information systems expert. One option would be to include a systems security expert and a network expert. Time is a crucial issue as well because it would take this small group of specialists several months.

Firstly, the group of experts must define the issues which fall within the interests of the drafter. In principle, apart from the legal issues several technical and security issues should be considered too. Afterwards, all the issues in question should be drafted into a single contract. This draft contract has to be put to trusted trade partners who should be asked to comment on it. Finally, it can be amended with respect to issues which have not been approved by the trade partners. Only then can the final interchange agreement be used. Although most self drafted agreements do not gain the trade partners approval, it is quite important that they do so. Such an approach can give more credit to the bilateral agreement and make it suitable for more wide scale use later.

All that comes at a price which, not surprisingly, can be quite high. Consequently, a trade partner who drafts its own interchange agreement can be described as a rather large EDI user with a high number of connections to make. The large volume of interchange agreements can moderate considerably the cost of drafting one. However, there are ways other than the number of trade partners which can help to scale down the cost. It is not always necessary to draft an interchange agreement from scratch. Instead one may choose to use a model agreement or one which has been already drafted as a basis. Anyway, it seems a difficult task for an SME.

5.3.2 Modification and Recycling of an Interchange Agreement

A small or medium sized user would probably prefer to use more cost efficient solutions. The trade partners can cut substantially in the budget for drafting their agreement if they choose to use a model agreement as a basis for their own draft. The major requirement in this case is to make the appropriate modifications to fit the particular needs of the users. The modifications can be for exclusive use but also others may use the modified product under licence. Organisations such as boards which supervise industrial or trade sectors can modify model agreements in a way that can serve the particular needs of the industry or trade. This technique can be best used among trade partners who are not in competition with each other or with regard to subsidiaries of a large user. The modification of an existing model agreement can better guarantee the legality of the amended model clauses and the uniformity in approach of the users to crucial issues. In the long run it can help the creation of customs in a particular sector of the market or industry.

Once an SME has prepared its own agreement it will have to negotiate in order to give it legal effect. Depending on the contents of the agreement, the proposed agreement may need revision. The endorsement of an agreement, either with modifications or not, depends heavily on the negotiating power of the parties.

In the next two sections we shall examine some of the points of friction in an electronic trade relationship. It is in the interest of the parties to limit the consequences of these conflicts and resolve problems at an early stage.

5.4 Contract Law Considerations

The introduction of EDI in business practice and the need to agree on interchange issues are factors which have to increase the awareness of parties with respect to clauses that contain hidden obligations on the parties and may result in loss or damage. Such issues are both commercial and legal in nature.

5.4.1 The Battle of Forms

When two parties start to do business together they exchange their general conditions of trade. In practice this may result in a misunderstanding about the actual rules which govern the transaction. In the paper based trade, parties exchange forms that contain contradictory terms sometimes. When in dispute, the parties can end up in court with respect to the validity and the legality of the terms of the transactions. The parties behave basically in the same way in the interchange agreement context as they do in a paper based transaction. They prefer to be the ones who keep the situation under their control, thus they impose their own terms on their business counterpart. Which party's terms will be vested with the power to regulate the inter-party relations is an issue left to be decided later.

It is quite important that the parties manage to agree on the transaction issues in question beforehand. The market position of the parties, for example, plays a significant role in defining their negotiating power. The negotiation of an agreement with a trade partner of equal market power may prolong the negotiations. It can be useful for the negotiations, but not necessarily fair, if a small trade partner approves an agreement which a large partner has proposed.

What trade partners usually do in practice is append their own transaction terms onto the interchange agreement. However, RM. Savage [85] believes that there are only a few issues to address in order to increase certainty and safeguard fairness in a transaction. Savage has drafted these issues in a comprehensive document which refers to the particular industry that his clients are involved in. It is quite clear that such an approach cannot always guarantee the level of fairness a trade counterpart would like to enjoy. Wright [85] has been critical of it by supporting the view that limitations of the trade partner's freedom to contract do exist. Thus, the agreement is not as fair as its drafter would perhaps like it to be. He concludes that it probably guarantees the same level of contractual freedom that can be found in many fully negotiated contracts.

In principle the party that proposes its terms last, is the ones whose terms prevail. It takes a carefully stated offer to manage to be the one whose terms govern the relationship. However important an issue, the battle of forms is not an issue that exclusively appears in the EDI context. It is just as important in paper based transactions. The parties may facilitate trade by directly referring to terms which have been exchanged electronically, and possibly agreed upon, at an earlier stage. In *American Multimedia, Inc. v Dalton Packaging, Inc.* [143 Misc. 2d 295, 540 N.Y.S. 2d 410 (sup. Ct. 1989)] the effectiveness of terms which were earlier transmitted was recognised. The fax stated that it was subject to certain terms which were already known to the parties.

5.4.2 Model Interchange Agreements and The Relations of The Parties

Recently, the European Commission within the TEDIS programme, published their own draft for a European model interchange agreement that has been adopted as a recommendation of the Commission of the European Union [15]. It is still too early to predict to what extent trade partners will actually make use of the model interchange agreements when trading with EDI. However, it should be made clear that a model agreement is no ready-to-sign document. The processed text requires quite some effort from the trade partners in order to make it fit their own needs. J. Ritter [62] commenting on the American Bar Association model interchange agreement notes that a model interchange agreement is an impartial document, free from any favouritism for one party or another. The agreement is no ready to use document. It leaves the parties the freedom to negotiate the final provisions of the clauses. However, it does cover the most important issues of the interchange.

To put it another way, there is only a very slim chance, if any at all, that model interchange agreements will be used as they now exist. This may contradict the intention of the drafters of the EDI model interchange agreements in attempting to provide the parties with an impartial tool. There are model agreements which are binding [9], like the NORSK and the UK EDI association agreements. There are others that encourage the trade partners to use their own judgement in relation to the final contents of the clauses, like the ABA model [9]. There is always a chance that when a party modifies a model agreement in order to make it fit the particular needs of its own trade, some undesired changes of the model provisions may occur. If this is the case, it is rather unlikely that the balance will be in favour of the party with the smaller negotiation power.

However, there is still some space for using a model agreement successfully. The fact that a model interchange agreement cannot be used as it is, must be viewed against the framework of unfair contractual clauses. Although a model interchange agreement seems to be difficult to use as it actually is, it still provides the parties with a fair and impartial regulation of their relations. A model agreement is in fact a "rightful regulation" of the relations of the parties. It has been drafted according to some rules and the issues it addresses are not in favour of one side or the other. In fact model agreements are not useful only to the weaker parties. They can also be useful to stronger ones. They can use a model agreement firstly, as a checklist of potential pitfalls and secondly, as a compass which will point to the direction of an acceptable regulation of the issues addressed. If any party, and especially the one who did not take part in drafting the agreement, has any suspicion about the fairness of the regulation he can always request its revision in court.

5.4.3 Legal Issues

The parties should be more aware of the following issues, which are crucial for the interchange. The forthcoming analysis has been mainly based upon the Draft Commission recommendation on a European Model EDI Agreement [15].

It is easy to start carrying out doing electronic transactions without taking any legal measures, such as signing a contract. It may work out all right for as long as everything goes well between the trade partners. However, if a party which feels that its interests are in danger has not agreed beforehand on certain legal issues as well as issues about the transmission, it can claim, that the transactions are not valid because they have been effected electronically and no hard copy of them has been retained. In such a case, see for example the electronic bills of lading, hard copies are necessary for the legality of an action. Such behaviour can have catastrophic consequences for the relations between the parties as well as for EDI transactions. The example demonstrates how vulnerable a trade party can be if it does not take a few precautions with respect to the legal issues of the transactions. Trust alone cannot help much in a crisis. Solutions can be sought on the basis of long standing procedures where trade partners have a well established relationship. This is not so with new trade partners who start to do business almost simultaneously with the implementation of EDI. In the light of open EDI, trust alone could cause damage if it is not accompanied by a clearly drafted agreement. The implementation of EDI hides legal dangers which the parties can resolve more easily if they can agree on a number of issues before commencing electronic transactions.

Validity, Formation and Evidential Value of an Electronic Contract

An example of the difficulty which electronic trade faces in respect to legal requirements is the requirement of writing. Even today, approximately twenty years after the introduction of EDI in trade practices, such matters have not been sorted out in all cases. There are, for example, particular types of contracts which have to be concluded in writing. Real estate contracts, for example, need notarial approval and they have to be entered in a public register [14].

In cases where such requirements are not necessary, like the transactions concerning movables for example, evidence requirements may cause unnecessary problems to EDI users. As long as the issue of the admissibility of electronic documents as evidence has not been regulated in most national legislations, it is usually the task of the judge to decide whether to admit an electronic document or not. However, a judge is not always bound by law to do so, even if a particular electronic document would appear to qualify. Thus, a piece of evidence may be rejected in court, if the judge thinks that electronic documents are unacceptable for evidential purposes. With respect to Common Law legislation, Tapper [77] suggests that automatic reproduction is real evidence not hearsay, thus admissible in an English Court. For Tapper the question is if the machine was working correctly at that time. This issue calls for the testimony of an expert witness. The question was put before a Canadian Court in *Queen v George & Hunter* [53] In this case the defendant was accused of trading in securities in order to create an artificial demand for securities, thus violating the Canadian Criminal Code. The Crown produced two kinds of print-outs: print-outs that detailed sales and purchase of shares summarising information kept by stock brokers and stock exchanges and computer printouts which were analyses that attempted to match purchases and sales. The Court held that the first kind of print-out was admissible because the primary source materials were in evidence. With respect to the analyses, the Court held that if a computer programme processes and interprets information to reach a conclusion which can be the subject of reasonable debate by humans, then the computer has produced an opinion which can only be presented by qualified witnesses. The Court required an expert witness who would adopt the material as his/her own evidence before the Court.

Until now national legislations have not explicitly considered technological developments with respect to the admissibility of electronic evidence. As long as such changes do not occur, trade partners have to address the issue in an agreement. Regulation of such a core matter by the trade partners themselves does not facilitate the application of EDI.

Liability for The Transmitted Data

The parties must make sure that they do not endorse any exclusion of liability clauses which can restrict their rights. The issue of the apportionment of liability for acts of the network operator demands special attention. This is an obscured issue in the relationships of the network operators both between themselves and with respect to trade partners. In principle, network providers tend to disclaim their faults by claiming that it is other parties, such as other network operators, who performed wrongfully in the transmission. The ever increasing level of liberalisation of the telecommunication services in Europe will result in the involvement of many parties in a simple transmission. The data will be handled by more than one network operator and it will flash in more than one network before it reaches its final destination. Thus, it can become extremely difficult to spot the exact point where the malfunction occurred and either prove the liability of the responsible party or apportion it fairly.

In continental legal systems there is usually a clause in the civil law codes that refers to the liability of contractors with respect to acts or omissions of intermediaries or their assistants (See for example, art. 278 of the German Brgerliches Gesetz Buch, art. 171 book 6 of the Dutch Burgerlijk Wetboek, art. 1384 5 of the Code Civile Francais, art 334 of the Greek Civil Code). However, when conducting trade internationally it is safer to include such a contractual clause as long as the legal provisions are not the same in all countries and the party who drafts the interchange agreement is not aware of the provisions of the legal system in the country of the counterpart. A common way to regulate the problem is to hold the party who has proposed the use of a particular network operator liable for acts or omissions the latter performs in the course of his duty. Such an arrangement can make it easier to prove the liability of a network provider. The parties must make sure that their agreement solves a problem in a straight forward manner. An interchange agreement usually contains a clause which limits the liability of the parties for damages suffered by the other party which were beyond the control of the former. These force majeure clauses are reflected in most model interchange agreements. Objective criteria for the apportionment of liability in electronic transactions would greatly assist the users. Insurance companies, which cover interchange losses, would also be interested in resolving this issue [34].

Dispute Resolution

If a dispute arises it is important that the parties have made arrangements beforehand in order to sort matters out before the situation becomes critical. The usual procedure is to take the dispute to court. Nevertheless, there are reasons why parties may prefer to avoid taking the dispute to court where there are certain drawbacks such as the publicly held procedure and the sometimes unreasonably long period before a decision is reached. Additionally, the trade partners may consider that the complexity of the application of EDI and the difficulty that lawyers and laymen usually face in understanding the legal problems related to technology may pose an additional barrier in bringing the dispute to court. Also, depending on the novelties incorporated in the particular application, parties may wish to avoid the publication of details of the application to competitors and other third parties.

Alternative dispute resolution (ADR) is a much more effective solution. Its use has been quite widespread among EDI users. The parties can reasonably expect to save time and money with the adoption of such a solution. The parties must make sure that the agreement on ADR does not harm their individual interests. De Mulder [19] suggests the use of a network operator as the mediator of disputes that arise from EDI transmissions. Such decisions could then go into appeal and could be heard in court.

The parties also need to determine the national law covering their transactions and which court has jurisdiction for the resolution of their disputes. Agreements which focus on intra border transactions work with the national law. However, for international transactions the parties have to agree on a legislation which offers an in-depth understanding of electronic trade issues. Unfortunately, as has been noted [9] there is not as yet any jurisdiction which regulates positively and understands thoroughly the issues of the interchange.

Protection of Personal Data

The protection of personal data is an issue of particular interest to trade partners who effect international transactions. Personal data protection is about the interests of a third party that is somehow involved in the exchanged information. Any agreement on data protection must comply with the national legislation of the country of the transmitting as well as the receiving party. Even though personal data protection is important, legal provisions do not appear to attract the attention of the general user. Thus the model agreements usually do not contain such clauses. So far there are only two model agreements that contain data protection provisions:

- The Quebec model agreement (art. 5.7) that calls for compliance with the provisions of the relevant Act (LQR, cA-2.1, Loi sur l'acces aux documents des organismes publics et sur la protection des renseignements personnels) for data transmitted by public organisations.

- The draft European model EDI agreement (art. 7.4) which dedicates a clause to data protection with respect to transmissions of data by senders or receivers who are established in a country where no such legislation exists.

However, not every country has personal data protection legislation. A corporate user who operates from a country with no such legislation can possibly damage a trade partner of a country which already has it, if the former does not agree to comply with it. In the case of transactions with trade partners based in countries with no such legislation, the European model EDI agreement provides the adoption of the Convention of the Council of Europe (Convention No. 108 of 28 January 1981) on the protection of the individual with regard to the automatic processing of personal data. A European Commission directive on the matter is also underway.

5.4.4 Technical and Business Issues

There are also a number of important technical and business issues which need to be considered by the trading parties before they commence any EDI transaction.

Transmission Standards

A fundamental issue upon which the trade partners have to agree is the transmission standards they plan to use. There are different kinds of transmission standards. The two used most widely are the UN/EDIFACT and the X12 standard, the latter is mainly used in the US whereas the former is more popular among businesses in Europe and the Far East. However, there are two constrains to consider, firstly. One is an open trade environment and the number of versions of the same standard. Steel [71] summarises the problem with standards in the following points:

- When a particular version of a standard is updated the users tend to keep the old one.
- Every industry produces implementation guidelines implementing the standard in its own way. Instead there should be a generic rule based structure to help the implementation.
- All this results in a myriad of implementations of versions of EDIFACT and X12.

TEDIS has recognised EDIFACT as well as standards approved by CEN and ISO as an interchange basis. However, the parties need to sort out the issue of updates and implementation. They have to see if they can agree upon using the same transmission protocol platform. If not, they need to make arrangements in order to resolve comprehensively upcoming issues. Where different standards are used, and the parties do not want the burden of providing themselves with translation software, they will probably have to include the issue in an agreement signed with their respective network operators.

Processing of Messages

When an EDI message reaches the computer system of the receiver it must be processed and its contents executed. According to the European model EDI agreement the parties may specify the time limits of their response (art. 5.1) in the Technical Annex. An obligation set down in a self drafted agreement with a too short process/execution period for the other trade partner can cause controversy. If, in addition, it permits the drafter to enjoy longer response periods, the arrangement can be ruled unfair. The parties must take all the necessary steps in order to agree on equal obligations in respect to the acknowledgement of the messages received. The parties have to pay special attention to the issue if they implement a fully automated system which excludes the use of human intervention. Forcing the in-house procedures of one party onto the other may result in delays in the implementation because of the adjustment time which will be required. The parties must also make sure that they agree on the compatibility of the procedures.

Security of Messages

Security refers to the general framework of the interchange and it does not concern the actual contents of a message. The latter is subject to the confidentiality provisions. It is not only the obvious case of confidential information transmitted over the network which attracts the attention of the drafters of an interchange agreement. Information apparently of a non-confidential nature can also disclose secrets about trade procedures and such which the transmitting party would rather avoid. On the one hand, the parties have to make sure that they agree to avoid all unauthorised transmissions. On the other hand as Wright [85] points out, that information may alter unintentionally. This can happen in two cases. Firstly, while it is translated from one format to another and secondly, while it flashes in more than one networks. In some cases the network provides an error detection and correction facility. However, even in this case the users are recommended [79] to take special measures in the case of data conversion, like to apply hash totals on amounts. The parties have to agree on the level of security which has to be maintained at a "commercially reasonable level" [9]. They must also ensure that the agreement imposes equal obligations for both parties concerning the provision of security procedures and ensuring the integrity of the messages. In particular the control measures must include checks, acknowledgement of receipt, control count, reference number, identification, digital signatures for sensitive data etc. When they detect a breach of security, the parties must be obliged by the agreement to inform the other party without further delay.

Confidentiality

The encryption of a message refers to its contents. The parties must make sure that they agree on the non-disclosure of the information which is considered to be confidential either unilaterally or bilaterally. Non-disclosure may include all third parties who are not familiar with the usual course of the transactions. The parties may agree upon the use of an encryption method which can guarantee the integrity of the messages they interchange.

The trade partners may agree on the following issues in order to assure the confidentiality of the exchanged information:

- Agreement that the information will be used only for the purposes agreed upon beforehand.
- Notification of personnel concerning the confidentiality of the information and for non-disclosure to third parties.
- Notification of the trade partner concerning the confidentiality of the information.
- Notification of the network operator concerning the confidentiality of the information.
- Notification of any third parties to whom the information is disclosed concerning the confidentiality of the information. In this case the same level of confidentiality as in the original transmission is required.

Operational Requirements

Standards and equipment for the implementation of EDI can both cause controversy. Hardware and software platforms are essential to EDI applications. If a particular model or version is no longer compatible, a trade partner may face problems when starting business with some other party. Multiplicity in the use of standards in EDI applications is also common. Some trade partners, try to tie their trade partners to that standard when they begin trading. If they do not provide data translators, it can be very difficult for the trade partners to begin EDI transactions with third parties. Trade partners with a dominant position in the market can undermine the position of the weaker trade partners.

The agreement on the provision of a network operator can also be an issue causing friction. Usually, trade partners do not have a direct point to point connection. They make use of the services of a network operator. Trade partners have to find their own operators and make arrangements directly with them in a separate deal. Trade partners with a strong market position who run their own proprietary networks have a dual function in the market. They are trade partners and network operators at the same time. Thus, they could potentially cause problems to the average user by imposing unfair regulations. The issues in question may cover the fields of provision of hardware and software equipment, maintenance of the system, renewal of equipment, functional specifications of the software and the like. If, together with the introduction of EDI, a party also makes an installation agreement, the trade partners may also consider attaching a hardware or software contract for the provision of the equipment with a detailed description of equipment and maintenance plans.

5.5 Some Competition Law Considerations

The activities of the trade partners can also be of interest from a competition law point of view. Competition considerations in the context of EDI still have a secondary effect although the deregulation of telecommunication services and the complexity this will bring should alarm the trade partners as to possible consequences on their trade relationships. It is predicted that deregulation will result in the appearance of more network operators and will multiply by several times the number of the value added service providers in Europe. The increased economic interest for the sector is expected to heat up competition.

In the case of a corporate trade partner who introduces or already uses EDI for his/her commercial activities there can be questions about the legality of these services in relation to European competition legislation. Economic strength leads to the desire to dominate the market and maximise profits. Apart from methods which can lead to price fixing policies, large users may also find other ways to mistreat their trade partners. Particularly when trade involves the development of intellectual property rights, trade partners may be tempted to exclude individual users or categories of uses from their products or charge more for their services. The merger of network providers with large users may lead to better economic results. The development of proprietary networks and the boost of technology may grant under certain circumstances an exemption from the regulations but it may also hide pitfalls.

Huet [30] draws analogies from a case of a prohibited agreement between airliners, which aimed to control a larger part of the market by attempting to link the reservation information systems of the companies. In its ruling in 1990 the Department of Justice of the US refused to approve the attempt of Delta and American Airlines to merge their information systems. The Commission of the EU has compiled a code of conduct on the subject and has issued a regulation in order to prevent such agreements with respect to breaches of article 85 of the Treaty of Rome.

5.5.1 Bottleneck Monopoly

Developing a standard communications protocol is quite a common activity among the trade partners who introduce EDI. Nevertheless, it is a time consuming and resource demanding activity. Thus, it can be quite hard for smaller trade partner to compete and develop their own. Small EDI users may find comfort in joining an industrial sector or association standards developing scheme. If the association develops its own standards or buys the rights to use one or more ready-made standards which are already used in the market for intellectual property rights, it can be difficult for trade partners who are not on good terms with the association or are ineligible for membership to develop their own standard. Once the association starts to distribute the standard to its members it may find it hard to refuse to provide it to an outsider user. Demanding unreasonably high fees for its use can have negative consequences.

In a similar case, the Commission took action against IGR Stereo Television from which it is easy to draw analogies to a case applied in EDI. Korah [36] reports on the case that:

> A trade association representing the German manufacturers of stereo TV sets acquired the patent rights for two rival technologies for making these. It then granted licences to its members, but refused one to the Finnish manufacturer, Salora, which was already operating on the German market. The Commission closed its file only when the association agreed to grant it licences too. Three years later, the Commission reported that the licence fees charged were too high and it intervened again to persuade the parties to reduce the royalties.

5.5.2 Collective Discrimination

In some cases, traders prefer to collaborate through trade associations. In the Benelux region for instance, trade ssociations tend to be huge involving many classes of vertically involved traders. The rules are strict for trade between members of the association and members and non-members. The aim is to form vertical trade chains all the way from production to retail. Thus, it becomes hard for a non-member to trade, due to the fact that from the import or the production all the way to the distribution and the retail the non-member stands alone. The European Court of Justice in a 1980 decision condemned such practices although it distinguished selective distribution. Korah [36] notes that:

> The Court It clearly distinguished its case law on selective distribution, whereby an individual brand owner may restrict dealers from selling to traders who lack appropriate premises and staff from collective agreements, whereby all manufacturers collectively set and apply the criteria, although later cases have ignored this important distinction.

A similar attitude of collective exclusion from the use of an interchange standard can be seen in the case of EDI. A national trade association which owns the rights to more than one standard can easily turn that into a competitive tool in order to restrict the entry of new traders who can potentially harm the interests of its members. Licensing the use of the standard only to members can leave others out of the market.

Admittedly, trade associations can have a positive influence on SMEs for as long as they can help them compete more effectively. In fact a trade association encourages competition and protects the market position of its members. However, there are cases in which an association has begun to act independently and competes on equal terms to its members. According to Triantafyllakis [66] in such a case abuse of a dominant position may occur. With respect to EDI and the future of networking, a dangerous move would be if the dominant users of EDI services join forces in order to gain an oligopsony position in the market. Their advantage could be even stronger if they could profit from the reductions which the network operators can offer for major users of the systems.

5.5.3 Technical and Economic Progress

The strong market position of many EDI users, if combined with the changes which are occurring in the telecommunications services, may substantially increase the power many of them have. Developments in technology make the open EDI an even more possible application. However, proprietary networks die hard and they can still offer particular advantages to their main users. The need to develop proprietary networks can lead to the merger of large users with service providers. This sort of development may result in undesired consequences for those trade partners who are the ultimate consumers of the services. The term consumer in this context is different from the end user of a product. Korah [36] notes that the term refers rather to end users in a greater sense of business rather than to the consumers of an everyday product. Thus, commercial law and competition law regulations apply instead of consumer protection ones.

The position of the main trade partner upon whom several others depend can become even stronger with the provision of multiple services. The multiplicity of the co-operation which the stronger parties can offer, extending from usual trade to network service provision, requires the determination of their legal position.

Closely related to such an option is the exemption from the competition regulations of concentration on the grounds of the development of technologically advanced products. According to the paragraph 1.b of the regulation 4064/89, which is based on the article 85 par. 3 of the EEC Treaty, exemptions can be granted for mergers which advance technological developments and therefore the benefits outweigh the undesired effects on the consumers from the irregularities of the applications of the competition policy. Such a case cannot be ruled out for as long as EDI applications are considered to be novel. In an attempt to foresee the community policies after the introduction of the above mentioned regulation Rounis [63] notes:

> The question is to what extent the Commission has the power under certain circumstances i.e. in order to assist the technological and economic developments, to approve merges which under different circumstances would be contrary to the common market, and additionally it can influence the progress of the industry within the EU.

The Commission has the power to decide on these matters alone, so the question is on which criteria the decisions will be effected. According to a statement in a 1989 report [55]:

> The Commission believes that the terms technical and economic development must be used according to the principles of the article 85 par. 3 of the Treaty and the decisions of the Court.

If exemptions start to be granted, the consequences of a deviation from the spirit of the legislative provisions could have quite a strong impact on European competition practice. It still remains to be seen whether legislative provisions have an actual effect on the decisions of the Commission.

5.5.4 Unjustified Refusal to Contract

Article 86 paragraphs (c) and (d) of the Treaty regulate the fundamental issue of an unjustified refusal to contract. The issue in question is prohibiting a trade partner, who holds a dominant position in the market, from abusing its position by refusing unjustifiably to contract altogether or by imposing conditions which the other party cannot fulfil. The latter case is an actual refusal. Papanicolaou [56] relates the effect of the refusal to the value which the goods have for the consumer or the user. He believes the only safeguard to be the limitation of the economic activity and consequently the contractual freedom of the stronger party. As a result, the weaker party could be reinstated in its rights. This kind of regulation of the relations of the parties can be better justified in the absence of an alternative solution for the weaker party, that is some other trade partner who would be willing to contract with the weaker one.

It is rather unlikely that there will be a large scale application of these provisions. There are suggestions, however, which call for the extension of the effect of necessary contracts (contrat necessaire) to the contracts signed for the provision of public goods and services. M. Wolf [56] relates the unjustified refusal to contract with the acceptance by the weaker party of terms which do not refer to the main scope of the contract but instead consist of derivative obligations. The acceptance of such an option could actually deprive the weaker one of its right to turn to another provider and therefore it reduces competition. The limitation of the economic freedom of a trade party has already had a negative effect on its activities. The ratio of the regulation is to make good to a certain extent the inequality of the parties. It is certainly not intended to be a form of "punishment" of the stronger party for its activities.

5.6 An Alternative Approach

The development of EDI at a technical level calls for changes in the approach of the users towards interchange agreements. Open systems will eliminate the possibility of negotiations before the transactions. Interchange agreements have proved to be useful so far. However, it is doubtful that they will be in the future. The ever increasing level of deregulation in the telecommunications sector will make matters more complicated for the users of EDI. An example showing the limits of the interchange agreements is the disclaimers of liability by the service providers. The parties have to accept responsibility for the actions of the network operators they propose to use as long as the latter disclaim any liability for their actions. Baum [6]suggests that:

> This problem has been exacerbated by communications industry deregulation, because multiple entities may participate in the establishment of a communications link.

The non-binding nature of the model interchange agreements is a point for consideration. Another one is the general legal approach they adopt. Most model agreements are not drafted in order to be used in a particular sector of the trade or industry. They are a set of rules good for the general EDI user. Thus they leave out special problems related to the implementation of EDI in any particular case. They cannot deal with other pre-existing commercial agreements which have been signed by the trade partners. If they take commercial issues into consideration, their approach cannot be detailed because it is impossible to refer to the numerous different ways in which trade partners conduct their business. Model agreements can only regulate successfully legal issues regarding the interchange. The business issues are usually drafted in a separate contract which is appended to the interchange contract. It is important, however, to link the interchange issues with the underlying transaction issues.

An interchange agreement cannot provide adequate protection for the signatories. It is unlikely that trade partners will give up the right which has been established in practice to draft whatever agreements they like in the way they prefer. It seems unlikely that the parties will ever accept the large scale use of model agreements as a replacement of the self drafted ones. Electronic trade must move towards other ways of regulation in order to expand and attract new users.

5.6.1 Binding Rules in A Model Interchange Agreement

Technology moves towards new business applications developments but the response of the legal world is not always prompt and accurate. In the light of new developments in trade practices, such as open EDI, model interchange agreements have to undergo changes in order to keep in line more effectively with the new situation. There are cases for which binding legal rules are important. Boss [9] reports that in the US there is a pilot industry-based EDI project which aims to establish direct relationships between manufacturers and retailers thus bypassing wholesalers. She points out the need for uniformity in the legal approach to EDI by suggesting that a binding agreement, which will be signed by a large number of retailers, is necessary for the success of the project. She notes that:

> For this project to succeed, a high degree of uniformity is needed in order to "deliver" to the manufacturers an acceptable volume of retailers. Moreover, there is a strong need for a model agreement with few opportunities for the parties to introduce variations.

There are cases where the problem has received proper attention. There are at least two agreements the contents of which are binding for their users . The NORSK agreement and the UK EDI association agreement are not supposed to be used as a basis for further development but rather to be used as they actually stand. The advantage of such an approach is that it can help the development of common trade practices.

5.6.2 A Code of Practice

If interchange agreements have a relatively small impact on addressing the real problems of the trade partner relationships, the task of helping the users could be undertaken by the users associations. Wright [86] reports that the Electronic Commerce Australia (formerly EDI Council of Australia) has adopted a Code of Practice. It addresses the most crucial legal issues posed by EDI in a quick and effective way and deal promptly with the needs of the trade partners. The latter can take action themselves by incorporating the provisions of the Code of Practice into other documents they produce. The Code is an impartial document which urges the parties to incorporate its guidelines into their own documents.

With respect to liability for example, the Code of Practice suggests that the parties should first seek an amicable solution and if that fails they should proceed by a mediated solution by a third party approved by the ECA. The Code does not enter into the contents of the exchanged message but instead it deals more with the message itself and its proper transmission. By approving the Code of Practice the parties grant authority to the ECA to intervene in the case of a dispute. In this case the Code provisions prevail and the ECA is responsible for providing the means to resolve the problems.

It is of paramount importance to ensure that any proposed solution either a model agreement or a Code of Practice or any other solution, must conform to the principles of fairness and openness. It will be even more difficult, however, to make the parties involved in electronic transactions curb their desire to maximise profits by using new technology within these limits. Fair legal solutions could promote the much needed widespread use of EDI. An attempt such as the Code of Practice of the ECA or a standard agreement which could be widely and unconditionally accepted and not subject to modification, could be an acceptable solution for trade partners.

The proposed Code of Practice could fulfil the needs of trade partners, particularly the smaller and weaker ones. The use of a Code of Practice, however, should not be kept restricted within national boundaries. Trade partners can benefit from the formation of regional EDI trade links and effect common interchange rules at a regional level. Consequently, common and fair interchange rules will promote more effectively the use of electronic trade.

A Code of Practice, if viewed in a wider framework of EDI applications at an international level, can lead in the future to a general agreement concerning EDI. Trade or industrial boards which control or supervise particular sectors could give a great deal of help in that respect. Such an agreement could summarise the legal rules upon which EDI will be conducted. Universal respect for such rules will shift the burden of drafting an agreement from the trade partners to their representative boards and will promote fairness in the transactions.

5.6.3 Arguments Against A General Agreement

A general agreement on the legal rules of EDI cannot be a panacea if not supported by legislative changes in the respective countries. There are certain rules in many countries which are not clear enough to accommodate electronic commerce freely. So far the response of the law has been that such rules can be interpreted in a way suitable to facilitate electronic transactions. The law would appear to be not explicitly against electronic commerce, but it is not clearly in favour of it either. There is always the danger that legal rules will be interpreted in a way which does not favour electronic transactions. The law of evidence with respect to the admissibility of electronic documents is one example of the inability of the law to fully apprehend and give a prompt response to issues that arise from the use of modern business applications. Any general agreement could become ineffective if not supported either, by amendments in national legislatures concerning the issues in question or by an interpretation of existing rules in a way facilitating electronic commerce.

Binding rules, especially if they are proposed by industrial boards or similar organisations, could raise questions in respect to competition law. If a model agreement, for example, becomes the widespread standard among a large number of users who are all members of a trade association the users will have to accept any competition law implications such an agreement may trigger. That could be a problem if a binding model agreement is drafted by an association of trade partners and sets out a series of rules for its users and their trade counterparts with respect to the transaction and the underlying commercial agreement.

5.7 Conclusion

If the stronger parties in a trade relationship abuse interchange agreements either by drafting unfair agreements or by abusing their market position and showing very little respect for the rights of their counterparts, it must be possible to regulate their activities without ending up in court. It is understood, however, that it is not easy to prevent a stronger party from abusing its superior negotiating position. Usually what trade parties seek is to increase their volume of trade by increasing the number of their business partners. Baker [5] notes that:

> Most companies have mixed motives when they try to negotiate EDI trading partner agreements. On one hand, they want to protect themselves against legal actions, particularly the kind that result from misunderstanding. At the same time, they don't want to be so protective of their own interests that they scare off potential trading partners.

If a trade partner abuses its relatively stronger position there could be direct consequences for the company, which could see the number of the trade partners decreasing. It is unlikely, that any company would like to see a potentially successful business innovation turn from a tool that increases the competitiveness of a company, to a boomerang that would harm its interests. However, the stronger the market position the more likely it is that an abuse of an interchange agreement occurs. The higher the level of dependence of the smaller trade partners on their stronger counterparts the more vulnerable they become. Therefore, they would grant their consent for the imposition of unfair terms.

Trade partners can gain more from the quick implementation of fair electronic trading rules. Interchange agreements, although useful in the earlier days of EDI, seem to be less effective as EDI changes. A solution should be sought in the direction of commonly accepted rules at a national or, even better, at a regional level which would be supervised by an approved independent third party. The trade partners can reasonably expect a decrease in the entry barriers and the disputes concerning the interchange. The parties can also expect that fair trade will promote trade efficiency.

Note: The author is a European Union research fellow.

Chapter 6

Advanced Electronic Commerce Security in a Workflow Environment

Hitesh Tewari, Maurice McCourt, Donal O'Mahony[1]

6.1 Introduction

Electronic Data Interchange is the process by which organisations exchange structured documents in electronic form. In the past, the focus of this technology has been on the mapping of information held in one companies internal information systems to an internationally standardised intermediate form suitable for electronic transmission to a business partner. Workflow technology, on the other hand, has focused on information flow within an enterprise and is concerned with the accurate tracking and routing of information as it is processed by individuals within an organisation. When these techniques are used in the context of electronic commerce, the possibility of fraud perpetrated by individuals outside of, or internal to an organisation becomes a very real possibility and consequently the use of security techniques becomes essential.

The EDI auditing and control workbench is an attempt to integrate the technologies of EDI, workflow and security to allow effective electronic commerce to take place from document production through to authorisation and transmission. Throughout a document's lifecycle, appropriate security techniques need to be enforced and adequate logging information maintained to satisfy the demands of both internal and external auditors. In section 2 of this document, we describe the functionality provided by the workbench, while section 3 concentrates on the security techniques used to enforce effective authorisation of documents

6.2 The EDI Audit and Control Workbench

6.2.1 Overview

EDI has an impact on the business processes employed by the trading partners, which, through proper business re-engineering, maximises productivity, quality

[1]Networks and Telecommunications Research Group, Department of Computer Science, Trinity College, Dublin 2, Ireland. e-mail: Donal.OMahony@cs.tcd.ie

and service and reduces lead times in the supply chain. The traditional sectors that have exploited EDI to date have been manufacturing and retail, which use EDI to achieve Just In Time (JIT) production and delivery. This, among other factors, has led to a 75% increase in manufacturing productivity in OECD[2] countries in the eighties. In the same time scale, office productivity has increased by only 3% [45]. What EDI does for inter business processes, workflow does for intra business processes. It makes sense therefore to examine means to integrate the two concepts.

Document authorisation within an organisation is a typical application that workflow handles well. In a paper based system, a paper document is initiated by someone, then evaluated and approved by others. The procedure maybe defined in a procedure manual, which states who has the authority to create and approve different categories of documents. In workflow systems, the procedure is automated. LAN technology is used to transfer the document in electronic form around the organisation. The route taken is typically defined at a central workflow server, which also maintains information about what actions a user may perform on the document, and indeed, which fields of the document the user may see or modify.

In this chapter we consider EDI document authorisation using a workflow environment which we will call an EDI Audit and Control Workbench. This is a distributed software system which will facilitate EDI document distribution using workflow techniques. The proposed system will be general enough to handle any office procedure requiring coordinated document distribution, but in this account we will focus on the procedure where a particularly sensitive EDI message, the Purchase Order, is produced. This requires an individual to create an initial purchase request, outlining the nature and purpose of the proposed purchase, and including details of the quotation to which it is responding (if appropriate).

The Workbench can analyse a request and route it dynamically according to specific field values (the total amount, say) for approval (with digital signatures) to the appropriate authorised participants in the workflow system. These participants may sign the document according to their 'signing power', or the amount for which they have authority to sign. When the request is approved, an EDI Purchase Order is generated and issued to the supplier signed with the organisation's private key.

6.2.2 How Workflow Works

A workflow system is a computer application system which models a *business process* by managing the flow of work among *participants*, according to a defined *procedure* consisting of a number of *tasks*. A job in a workflow system is known as a *case*. Workflow co-ordinates user and system participants together with the appropriate data resources, which may be held on or off-line (i.e. on paper), to achieve defined objectives within specified time constraints. The co-ordination

[2] OECD - Organisation for Economic Cooperation and Development

involves passing tasks from participant to participant in correct sequence, ensuring that all fulfil their required contributions, and taking default actions where necessary [33]. Workflow models the organisation hierarchy based on roles rather than individuals.

In this example, the business process being automated is Purchase Order authorisation, which is defined as a procedure to the workflow system. Purchasers, Managers and Auditors are distinct roles played by people in the organisation. If person X has the role of a Purchaser responsible for purchases from a particular supplier, and X is temporarily unavailable, (e.g. sick, or on holidays), we can specify person Y to take his place, without having to redefine for Y the steps performed by X to manage orders for that supplier. In certain cases (especially in smaller organisations), it may be possible for an individual to be both a Purchaser and a Manager.

The role of Auditor is independent from the purchase cycle - i.e. an Auditor has no authority either to originate or approve purchases. His role is to ensure the efficiency and effectiveness of the system, and to prevent and detect fraud. He is responsible for the correct usage of the company's private signature. The Auditor should be a senior financial officer within the organisation.

The actions of each participant in the procedure are illustrated in Figure 6.1. A purchase request is created by a Purchaser and is treated as a case. The Manager's task is to assess the request and approve or deny it. For example, if the amount is for greater than $1000 but less than $10000 ('say), three Managers at level 1 in the organisation's hierarchy are required to authorise the request. Otherwise, for amounts greater than $10,000 the signatures of two Managers at level 2 are required. Finally, the approved request is converted automatically to conventional EDI Purchase Order format and sent to the supplier. If the Auditor is satisfied the system is running correctly, he need not examine every Order issued. He should be notified of exceptions, where a request is refused, or referred to him by a participant for assessment.

Work performed by participants in the system may be distributed according to the role categories defined. This distribution of work may use any algorithm deemed to meet the organisation's requirements. For example, the algorithm may poll participants in a fixed sequence, or alternatively it may use an 'available agent' approach. For example, a purchase request requiring a signature from two Managers may be signed by any two of n (where n>=2) Managers who are available to process the request. The workflow scheduler may request all available Managers at this level of the hierarchy to sign the request, accepting the first two "volunteers".

This summary of workflow concepts concentrates on those aspects relevant to the purposes of this chapter. A more complete treatment of workflow systems is given in [12] and [17].

6.2.3 Workbench Components

The EDI Audit and Control Workbench implements internal document routing using workflow techniques, leading to the generation of an authorised EDI

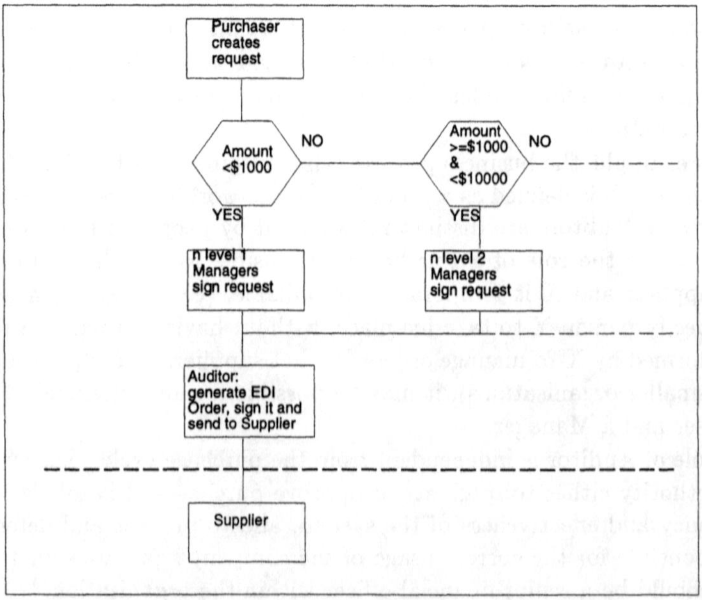

Figure 6.1 Roles in an Organization Hierarchy

message. A central workflow scheduler routes incoming or outgoing documents among participants on the basis of user defined rules, branching according to the value of specified fields in each document. A complete audit trail allows the status of documents to be tracked within the system.

The Workbench consists of a series of modules which may configured on a single machine, or distributed across a network. The following modules are specified (see Figure 6.2):

- a Workflow Scheduler which routes EDI messages among Workbench participants (which may be human, or other modules in the system);
- an Audit and Control module which performs automated integrity checks on message contents, and if the request is approved, creates a Purchase Order with the company signature. All sensitive information could be securely stored here (this module should be kept in a secure location under the close supervision of the Auditor);
- a Communications module to transmit and receive messages;
- a Security module which performs cryptographic functions on messages;
- a Record Keeping module to manage storage of messages according to a retention schedule. This should archive not only completed EDI messages, but also all intermediate states (including errors and exceptions) so that a comprehensive audit trail is available;

- an Administration module, from which the Workbench administrator can define workflow rules, record retention schedules etc.

Additionally, separate modules may be configured by the Workbench administrator according to the workflow role requirements e.g. a Message Viewing module, or a Message Authorisation module.

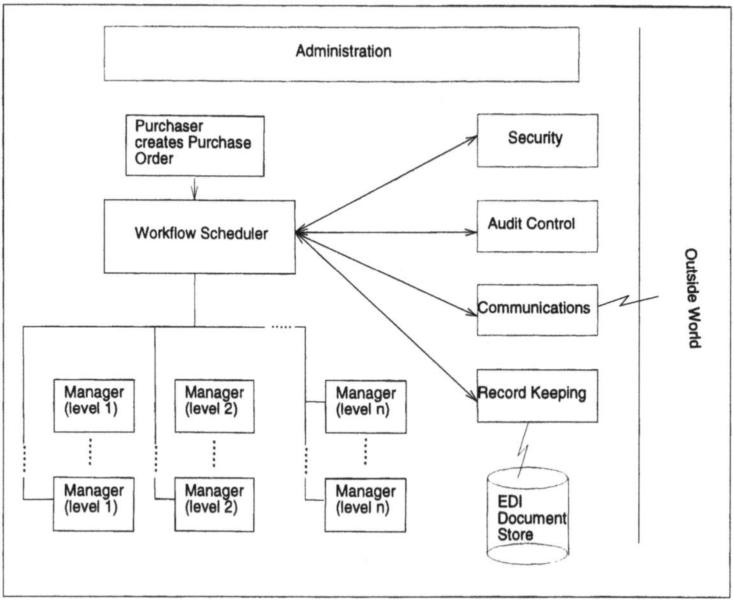

Figure 6.2 Workbench Architecture

The objective is to maximise the efficiency of internal authorisation procedures, and to trap unauthorised documents before the transmission point. This latter objective contrasts with the audit-by-receiver paradigms proposed by Fischer [24] and elaborated by Russell [65], where the message receiver (i.e. the supplier) would be given sufficient information about the senders internal approval structure to validate the message. These systems expose the senders personnel to breaches of privacy, and the senders organisation to attempts at personal corruption by avaricious vendors. The workflow system alleviates some significant grievances cited by auditors of EDP[3] systems [84] [18]. Visual control over the contents of the Purchase Order is restored to the humans responsible for the purchase. Also, significant segregation of duties is achieved - workflow roles distinguish between request originators, signatories and auditors, who each have independent powers of control.

However, the system does not assist suppliers who wish to establish that the received order has been properly validated by the sender, or that the sender has sufficient funds to pay for the purchase.

[3] EDP - Electronic Data Processing

6.3 Electronic Document Security

The central purpose of the system proposed in this chapter is to prevent fraudulent trade documents (EDI) being issued from an organisation. Documents must circulate securely via electronic means within the organisation and then outside to the trading partner. This is achieved using digital signatures based on public key cryptography, perhaps with an additional feature, control vectors, enabling secure off-line authorisation.

6.3.1 Structured Documents

In order to move electronic documents securely around a network, either within an organisation or between trading organisations, a document structure must be agreed.

Globally agreed open standards for structured documents within an organisation (i.e. workflow forms) do not as yet exist. Many proprietary electronic forms packages are available; however, we must specify the basic contents and structural requirements for a purchase request.

Essentially, a purchase request will contain the same fields as an EDI Purchase Order - the identity of the creator, a description of the goods being ordered, a reference to a quotation for the goods, the identity of the supplier, and security information. The quotation for the goods is important, as authorisation of the request is based on the total value of the request. The security information will consist of a list of one or more digital signatures, together with each signers public key certificate (see next section). Most forms packages include the ability to annotate a form with informal unstructured messages, a function which is useful for internal processing of a request.

Exchange of structured documents between organisations is achieved using Electronic Data Interchange (EDI). Two main EDI standards exist: UN/EDIFACT (a global standard) and ANSI X12 (used mainly in North America). The two standards are set to merge in the future, but currently there are some differences in implementation, notably in the area of security. At the time of writing, EDIFACT messages may use public key cryptography, whereas X12 may not [59]. Secure X12 therefore is restricted to closed trading partner relationships, where exchange of symmetric keys can take place.

The final Purchase Order need not include the quote for goods, but it is advisable to include this, as the receiver (the supplier) can then check that the Order was approved by the sender (the buyer) based on reliable information.

6.3.2 Public Key Cryptography

The notion of public-key cryptography was introduced by Diffie and Hellman [82]. Unlike the Data Encryption Standard [54], which is a symmetric key based algorithm, in a public key cryptosystem each user is issued a pair of keys, one for encryption and one for decryption. The encryption key is referred to as the *Public Key* (E) and may be kept in a public repository such as the X.500

Directory [13]. The decryption key, also referred to as the *Private Key* (D) is only known to the user to whom it has been issued. It is usually stored in a secure module such as a tamper-resistant chip card. The need for sender and receiver to share secret information is eliminated: all communications involve only public keys, and no private key is ever transmitted or shared. The algorithm ensures that knowledge of the public key should not be sufficient to allow someone to derive the corresponding private key. Public key cryptography, unlike symmetric key cryptography, can be used for authentication (digital signatures) as well as for privacy (encryption).

If Alice wants to send an encrypted message to Bob, she looks up Bob's public key in a directory, uses it to encrypt the message and sends it off to Bob. Bob then uses his private to decrypt the message and read it. No one listening in can decrypt the message. Anyone can send a message to Bob encrypted with his public key, but only Bob can read it.

To sign a message, Alice performs a computation involving both her secret key and the message itself; the output is the signature and is attached to the message which is then sent to Bob, to verify the signature. Bob does some computation involving the message, the purported signature, and Alice's public key. If the two signatures match then one can assume that the message has not been tampered with.

In practice however Alice would use a hash function to create a message digest, which serves as a "digital fingerprint" of the message. She then encrypts the message digest with her private key; this is her digital signature, which she sends to Bob along with the message itself. Bob, upon receiving the message and signature, decrypts the signature with Alice's public key to recover the message digest. He then hashes the message with the same hash function Alice used and compares the result to the message digest decrypted from the signature. If they are exactly equal, the signature has been successfully verified.

In a small cryptosystem where the number of keys is relatively few, key usage can be inferred from the key itself. But as the number of keys in the system increases, it becomes increasingly difficult to gauge key usage for a particular key. This can lead to incorrect use of keys and security breaches within the system. Thus the obvious need to find a mechanism to control key usage.

6.3.3 Control Vectors

The concept of control vectors was developed at IBM [46] and later implemented within IBM's Transaction Security System (TSS). The driving force behind the design was to control *key usage*, an area which has been largely overlooked in the past. This is achieved by associating with each key a set of key related information *(a control vector)* which spells out under what conditions the key can be processed by a cryptographic device. In addition the key related information is cryptographically *locked* with the key to prevent the control vector information from being changed. Figure 6.3 illustrates the internals of the cryptographic subsystem. It consists of a key storage facility which will store an individual's private keys, as well as any system wide keys. An instruction processor which will handle all the cryptographic processing and an optional transaction store which can be used logging and auditing purposes. A cryptographic subsystem such as the one described above can easily be implemented using currently available chip card technology.

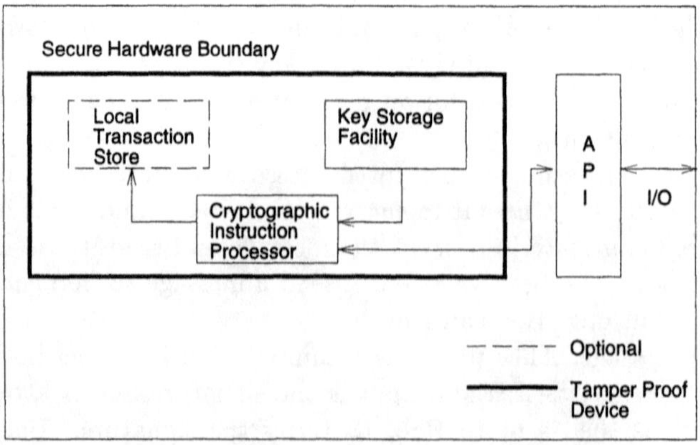

Figure 6.3 Cryptographic Subsystem

The control vector is a *nonsecret* cryptographic variable used by a key management scheme to control cryptographic key usage. The control vector is composed of a set of encoded fields representing the authorised or permitted uses of the key. The cryptographic system is designed such that key processing can be performed only if requested use of the key is authorised by the control vector. A key on the other hand is composed of a randomly generated string of 0 and 1 bits (assuming we are dealing with a symmetric key algorithm such as the Data Encryption Algorithm [4]). In addition to these two entities in the system, there are system wide keys which may be held at each site in the system. These are stored in tamper-proof modules and are inaccessible to the user. An example is the key-encrypting key (KK), which is a 64-bit DEA key used to encrypt users keys.

During key generation, the key and control vector are cryptographically coupled, to prevent the control information from being changed (otherwise, the key-usage attributes granted to each key could be changed by merely replacing one control vector by another). This involves encrypting the generated key K with a variant of the key-encrypting key of the form $KK \oplus C$, where $KK \oplus C$ is produced as the Exclusive-OR product of the key-encrypting key KK and control vector C. Upon recovery, the key-encrypting key is again combined with the control vector within the tamper proof module to produce the same variant key $KK \oplus C$. $KK \oplus C$ is then used to recover the key K. All cryptographic functions such as encryption/decryption and coupling of keys are performed within the cryptographic hardware.

This combination of key plus control vector is presented at the input of a secure hardware device (see Figure 6.4) which will apply the key only to operations permitted by the control vector. Note also that clear keys can never be

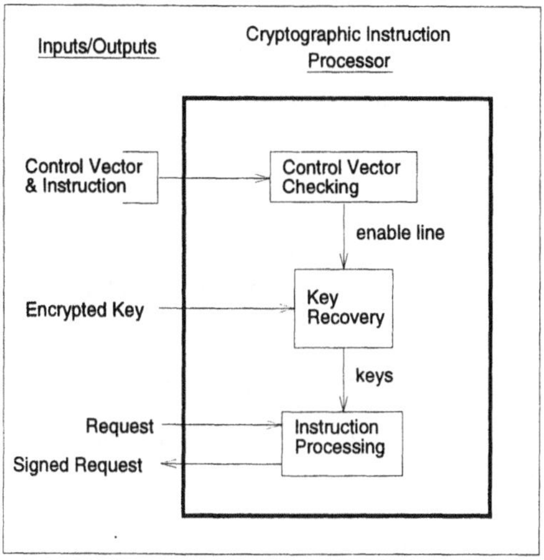

Figure 6.4 Control Vector Checking Process

recovered outside of the cryptographic hardware.

A control vector is produced using a user application program. The user supplies keywords/parameters which are encoded in the control vector as Manager fields. The key specifies the cryptographic algorithm to be used. The control vector customises the hardware instruction processor by selecting a subset of the possible instructions or instruction modes executable by the cryptographic software i.e., the control vector in effect prescribes the authorised uses of the key.

In a key management scheme using control vectors, each key (K), will have associated with it a control vector C, where K and C constitute a logical 2-tuple (K,C), K and C are coupled cryptographically. A simple way to achieve this is to integrate C into the functions used to encrypt and decrypt keys. Thus key K is recovered within a device only if the correct control vector is specified. Specification of an incorrect control vector will result in the generation of a spurious key. Various steps are taken during the coupling phase that ensures the above. The algorithms used to encrypt and decrypt a key are called the *Control Vector Encrypt* (CVE) and the *Control Vector Decrypt* (CVD) algorithms respectively. The exact details of each of the algorithms can be found in [46].

The above concept can also be used for key management schemes using asymmetric (public key) algorithms. Figure 6.5 shows a typical control vector. The key-encrypting key will still be a 64-bit DEA key, while the public and private exponents will be 512-bit RSA [60] keys. The *CV Type* field indicates whether the key is a public key, a private key or a key management key. The *Usage Attributes* field indicates the cryptographic services in which the key can be used. The *Algorithm* field indicates the algorithm with which the key can be used. The *TStart* (i.e., starting time) field and the *TExp* (i.e., expired time) field together indicate the validity period of the key.

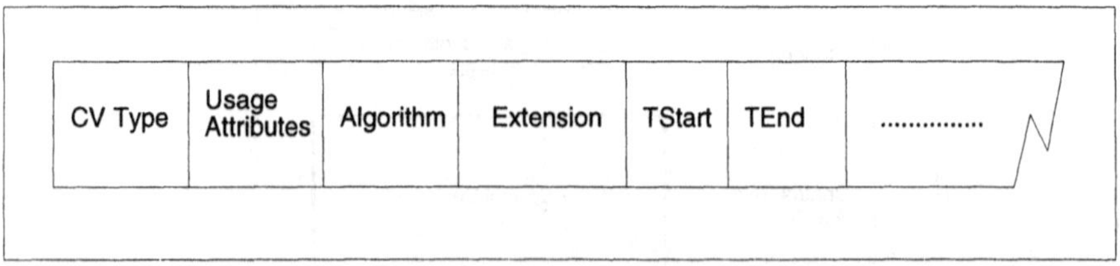

Figure 6.5 Control Vector Fields

6.3.4 Enhancement of Signing Power

As described earlier, a single purchase/payment order may have to be signed by more than one person (multiple signatures) before it can be approved by the finance office. Generally, the amount will be small enough for one or more lower level authorities to approve the order. In some cases signatures from Managers higher up in the organisation is needed. In order to avoid unnecessary routing of the request *up* through the organisation hierarchy, it may be routed *across* at the same level.

Our protocol exploits the concept of *Enhancement of Signing Power*. A Manager on his own may be able to sign a document for an amount **X** (his Single Limit Approval - SLA). In collaboration with n of his peers he may sign the same document for a higher amount **Y** (the Multiple Limit Approval - MLA) which may be greater than the sum of each Manager's signing power (i.e. $\mathbf{Y} > (n * \mathbf{X})$).

The hierarchical model of an organisation used here is simple but flexible. Managers are grouped into increasing levels of authority. Managers at each level have the same SLA and MLA values. However, a Manager may belong to more than one hierarchical level, thus increasing his range of signing power. A Manager may also be a Purchaser, empowering him to originate purchase requests.

The information about the amount for which a Manager (or a group of Managers) may sign is extremely sensitive. The protection of this information is central to the organisation's anti-fraud policy. The following sections outline two approaches to the protection of this information. The first uses a secure, centralised database. The second employs a novel approach using control vectors.

6.4 The Secure Database Scheme

In the case where a centralised approach to authorisation is taken, all routing information is stored in the Workbench's Audit Control Module. This module maintains a physically secure database containing a control table of participants and the amount limits for which they may sign. This data corresponds to the private data shown in Figure 6.6. This data must be maintained in a secure database to ensure that a fraudster may not alter his/her purchasing limit.

The Workbench facilitates this by permitting the Audit Control Module to be run anywhere on the organisation's network, under the close supervision of the Auditor. The Module also contains all cryptographic hardware and software for the system.

Manager Level	Single Limit Approval SLA	Multiple Limit Approval MLA	Number of Participants NP
1	100	1000	4
2	1000	10,000	3
3	10,000	100,000	2

Figure 6.6 Control Table

When a purchaser creates a purchase request, he submits it to the workflow scheduler which sends it to the Audit Control Module. The Module creates a rule R for authorisation of the message based on the amount value of the request and the information in the control table of participants. R consists of the number n of signatures required, and a list of m participants who may sign the message. Of course, m must be equal to or greater than n.

The Audit Control Module returns the request and the rule R to the workflow scheduler, which processes the rule according to an algorithm suitable to the organisations requirements. For example, it could send a message to all m participants in R asking them to respond if they are available to sign the request. The scheduler sends the request to the first n participants who are available to sign the message.

When the scheduler has gathered the required signatures, the signed request is returned to the Audit Control Module, which evaluates it, and checks that the requirements of the rule R have been fulfilled. The Audit Control Module generates an EDI Purchase Order with a single company signature, and returns the Order to the scheduler for routing to the EDI Communications Module for delivery to the Supplier.

Exceptions, such as the refusal of a manager to sign an request, or the detection of an error executing the control rule, are stored at the Audit Control Module, and an alarm is generated.

Note that the role of the scheduler is quite straightforward - the request is simply routed from one participant to the next, without being parsed or validated in any way. Also, the digital signatures created with the authorising participants smart cards are conventional public key signatures on the message stream - no request validation is performed with the card. Message control in the centralised scheme is performed solely within the Audit Control Module.

6.5 The Control Vector Scheme

In the previous scheme the *Audit Control Module* was the central decision making body. It was envisaged to contain a secure tamper proof database which held control tables, based on which it made its decisions. On the other hand this central model allowed no local control over what a Manager could or could not sign for on behalf of the organisation. In contrast to that approach the following scheme has a more distributed thread of control, at the same time strictly controlling a Managers signing power, which is achieved with the aid of control vectors.

6.5.1 Extensions to the Control Vector

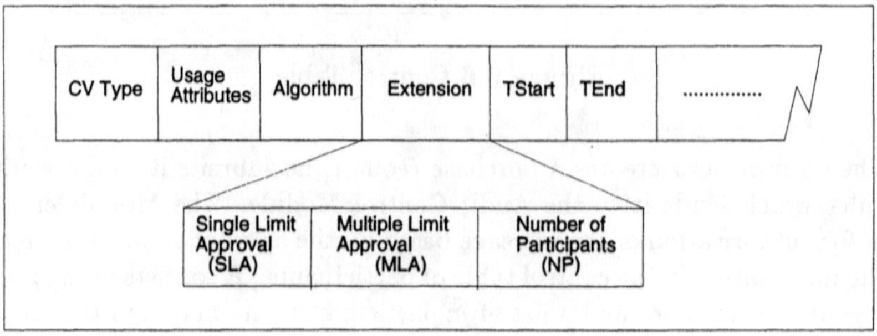

Figure 6.7 Extensions to the Control Vector

In this scenario, the control vector has been extended to incorporate fields which will be used in our protocol, see Figure 6.7. The *Single Limit Approval* (SLA) field indicates the amount for which the Manager has authority to approve a document. The *Multiple Limit Approval* (MLA) field indicates the amount the Manager has authority to approve in collaboration with n of his peers as defined by the Number of Participants (NP) field in his control vector.

Each of these fields will be checked by the cryptographic instruction processor before creating a digital signature. If the Manager's SLA is insufficient for him to approve the document alone, he may still sign the document (if the *total amount* is less than his MLA) which will enable document approval with NP-1 of his colleagues.

6.5.2 Protocol Specification

The main participants in our protocol are the users within the organisation, the workflow server and the suppliers. The users may consist of purchase personnel, managers and senior managers etc. The basic operation can be divided between two major entities in the system, namely the cryptographic subsystem and the workflow server. The cryptographic subsystem is concerned with creating digital signatures and ensuring that users only approve documents for which they have authority.

The workflow server on the other hand is concerned with the routing of the document through the organisation to Manager for authorisation. It must do this efficiently i.e., it must be able to get a document approved with the least number of signatures at the lowest possible authority level. The workflow scheduler has a rule set which defines the organisations internal hierarchy or the authority level of each Manager within their organisation. This rule set is not secret and need not be held in a secure area as we will see.

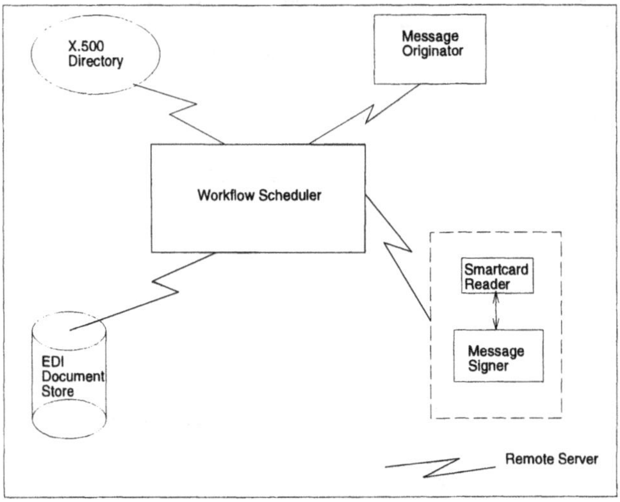

Figure 6.8 Overview of Control Vector Scheme

The basic scheme is shown in Figure 6.8. Each user in the system is issued with a chip card module which contains the cryptographic facility capable of processing control vectors and being able to perform a mapping between a set of structured documents and their associated value. In addition the cards key storage facility is loaded up with a number of user and system specific keys, namely:

- A Key-encrypting Key (KK) which is used in cryptographically coupling the users secret key with his control vector. This is a system wide key i.e., common to all users.

- A user specific control vector CV_{user} which is specifically configured for each user in the system. The users Single Limit Approval and Multiple Limit Approval fields are specified within the control vector (see Figure 6.6).

- The users private key cryptographically coupled with the users control vector $\overline{K_{s_{user}}}$. This key is used to sign a request which requires further authorisation.

- The company's private key cryptographically coupled with the user's control vector $\overline{K_{s_{comp}}}$, which is used to create a signed EDI Purchase Order that may be transmitted directly to the supplier. The supplier should be able to validate the Order with the company's public key.

- A certificate which contains the identity (ID) and the public key of the signer, and the expiry date (ED) of the certificate. These three fields are signed with the private key of the Certification Authority (CA). In addition the public key of the CA (K_{pCA}) is appended to the signature, so that participants can verify the signature. The format of a certificate for user A looks like the following:

$$C_{CA}(A) = ID_A, ED_A, K_{p_A}, sig_{CA}(ID_A, ED_A, K_{p_A}), K_{pCA}$$

Similarly, the signature for company *comp* appended to the Purchase Order looks like:

$$C_{CA}(comp) = ID_{comp}, ED_{comp}, K_{p_{comp}}, sig_{CA}(ID_{comp}, ED_{comp}, K_{p_{comp}}), K_{pC}$$

Smart Card Operation

When the workflow scheduler receives a request, it selects the managerial level at which the request should be authorised, based on the *total amount* field of the message. The scheduler selects one of the available managers (or participants) and passes the request to him. The selection algorithm used may vary according to organisational needs.

When a participant receives a document for approval from the workflow scheduler, he submits it to the cryptographic subsystem in his chip card (see 6.9). The cryptographic hardware is able to isolate *total amount* field of the purchase request and compare it with the Single Limit Approval (SLA) and Multiple Limit Approval (MLA) fields within the participant's control vector. It signs the document by creating a message digest on the message (M), the participants control vector (CV) and the Number of Signatures (NS) field. This field is contains a count variable which is incremented each time the card appends a signature to the request. This enables the cryptographic subsystem to deduce when the correct number of signatures have been acquired.

If the participant is the first person to sign the request i.e, the request contains no appended signatures, the cryptographic facility checks the *total amount* field against the Single Limit Approval (SLA) of the participant. If the participants SLA is greater that or equal to the *total amount* then the chip card creates an EDI Purchase Order (PO) signed with the company key. This is ready for direct transmission to the trading partner using the Workbench's communications module.

$$Sig_{COMP} = K_{s_{comp}}(C_{comp}, H(PO, C_{comp})$$

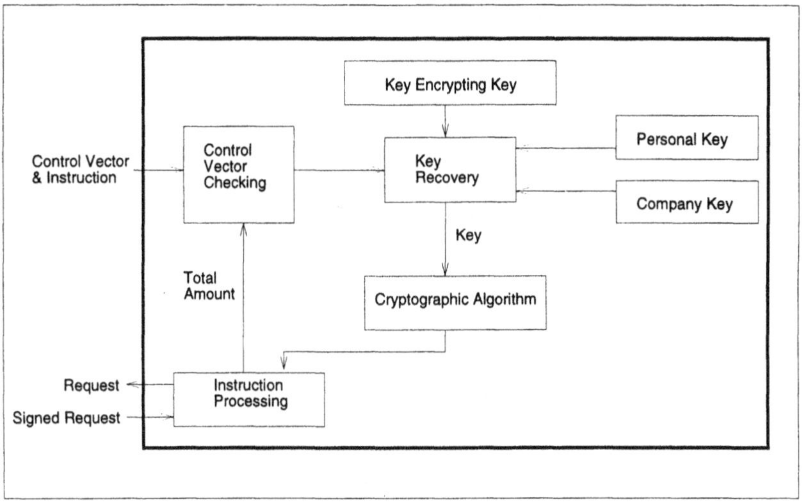

Figure 6.9 Architecture of the Cryptographic Subsystem

If the first participant cannot approve the document alone i.e., the participant's SLA is less than the *total amount* field within the request, the smart card creates a digital signature on the request with the personal key, and sets the NS field within the signature to one, specifying that the document has been approved by one participant.

$$Sig_A = K_{s_A}(C_A, NS, H(M, C_A, NS)$$

The digest along with the participant's control vector and the NS field are encrypted with the participants private key K_{sA}. In addition, the participants certificate $C_{CA}(A)$ will be appended to the end of the signature. This will enable the next smartcard which processes the request to validate the signature.

Alternatively if the participant is not the first person to sign the document then the card validates the last signature appended to the document, and notes the value of the NS field. The instruction processor compares the *total amount* segment with the Multiple Limit Approval (MLA) specified within the participants control vector. If the amount is less than or equal to his MLA, and the number of signatures NS is less than the number of participants NP-1, then a signature with the card's personal key is generated, with NS incremented by one. If NS in the validated signature is equal to NP-1, then all the required approvals have been acquired: an EDI Purchase Order is created from the request, and signed with the company key. This message is ready for direct transmission to the trading partner.

If the situation arises where the *total amount* of the request is greater than a participant's MLA, then a serious exception has occurred - this participant should not have received the request for approval. In this case, the workflow scheduler's organisational hierarchy table contains inaccurate information (it may possibly have been altered fraudulently). The Auditor in charge of the Audit Control Module is notified (see next section).

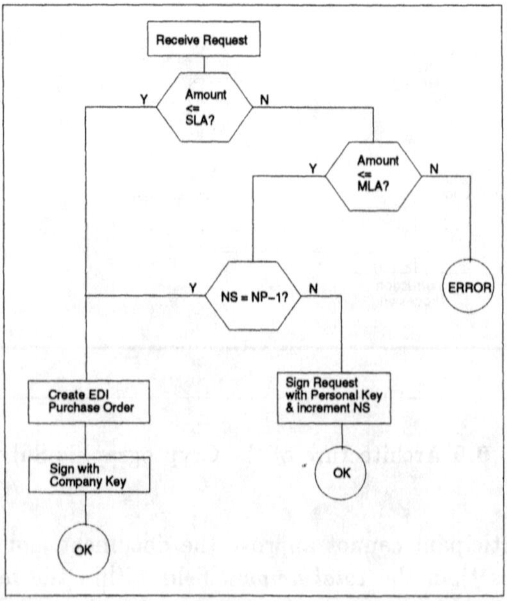

Figure 6.10 Request Approval by the Smartcard

Workflow Operation

The workflow server is concerned with routing the document within the organisation. The workflow does not hold any *state variables* and neither does it hold any secret information, such as Manager's single/multi limits, nor any cryptographic hardware or software. It does however hold a table which specifies the organisations internal hierarchy where Managers are organised into different authorisation levels as outlined in Section 3.4.

The workflow scheduler will thus route the document (using its internal routing tables) and will solicit approval of the document from Managers within the organisation. Each time the document is returned to the workflow scheduler, it will check if it is an EDI Purchase Order signed with the company key. If so, the message is forwarded to the Communications software for transmission to the trading partner.

If on the other hand the request is returned to the scheduler with an error message (i.e. the Manager will not or can not approve it), then it will send the document to the Audit Control Module which will notify the Auditor that an exception has occurred.

This scheme means that the amount of processing of the request required by the Workbench is significantly reduced - the smartcard protocol performs all of the request verification required - offline. The security of the system is enhanced, as the sensitive data, which, if altered could lead to fraud, is inaccessible on the smartcard.

6.6 Conclusions

We have presented the design for an EDI auditing and control workbench which can combine the use of workflow as a tool to control intra-enterprise documentation together with EDI as the means by which trade documents can be transferred between organisations. The security architecture outlined protects a company from the normal risks associated with electronic trading as well as providing some means of control over the 'signing power' allocated to employees of the enterprise. Keys issued to individuals are coupled with a control vector specifying the conditions under which the key can be used. By extending the control vector scheme with support from appropriate secure hardware modules, it is possible to allow an individual who ordinarily can only authorise a document at a given level to collaborate with employees at the same level to enhance this signing power to that of a higher level. This reflects existing practices within organisations when paper-based trading is in force.

Throughout all of the processing, explicit recognition is given to the requirements of both internal and external auditors. This is the final ingredient in a system that provides a firm basis for making the shift to true electronic commerce.

Chapter 7

Temporal Reasoning for Automated Workflow in Health Care Enterprises[1]

Ira J. Haimowitz[2], James Farley, Glenn S. Fields, Jonathan Stillman and Barbara Vivier

The current healthcare environment of consolidation and cost cutting is creating loosely coupled groups termed *virtual healthcare enterprises.* In order to control costs, manage information, and provide seamless care, these enterprises will benefit from *electronic commerce*: electronic distribution of many transaction types, including clinical, administrative, and financial. We view an essential component of electronic commerce in this context to be *automated workflow*: automating the flow of documents and related information through a business process. As part of a multi-year project within a multiple-site consortium called HOST (Healthcare Open Systems and Trials), we are developing tools for acquiring, representing, and simulating workflows for healthcare enterprises.

Lacking in current workflow tools is the crucial ability to model and track the time resources of tasks within an overall process. In this chapter we advocate and demonstrate explicit temporal reasoning for automated workflow. Through our temporal reasoner Tachyon, we show how temporal models of some healthcare processes may provide valuable information to clinicians, administrators, and patients. We also suggest extensions to Tachyon to capture the temporal aspects of workflow more expressively.

---

[1] This research was (partially) done under a cooperative agreement between the National Institute of Standards and Technology Advanced Technology Program (under the HIIT contract, number 70NANB5H1011) and the Healthcare Open Systems and Trials, Inc consortium

[2] All authors at General Electric Research and Development, P.O. Box 8, Schenectady, N.Y. 12301. Correspond to Ira J. Haimowitz, Building K-1; Email: haimowitz@crd.ge.com

7.1 Introduction

7.1.1 Problem: Linking Virtual Health Care Enterprises

In the United States several healthcare industry forces are creating *virtual healthcare enterprises*: loosely coupled healthcare groups consisting of geographically disparate entities with differing legacy information systems. Virtual healthcare enterprises are also termed *integrated delivery systems*. Despite their distributed nature, these enterprises need integrated administration and must provide seamless health care to patients.

Concurrently, the U.S. spends more of its Gross Domestic Product (14 percent) on healthcare than does any other industrialized country. Rising health costs drain resources away from other productive uses, threaten the competitiveness of American firms, add to the Federal deficit, and reduce national savings.

The resulting challenge is effectively integrating and coordinating the administrative, financial, and clinical processes associated with virtual healthcare enterprises, while controlling overall costs.

7.1.2 Current Health Care Commerce

The healthcare industry currently relies on people-intensive, paper-oriented processes augmented by "islands of automation" to address its administrative, financial, and clinical information needs. Patient records are almost entirely paper-based, hand-written entries. Clinical procedures require authorization paperwork. The preponderance of medical claims are paper-based (giving rise to an industry to convert paper claims to electronic form for processing by insurers). Purchasing, reporting, and other key administrative functions are largely paper-based processes. The term "islands of automation" refers to specific functions or domains within the hospital or practice that are automated – largely consisting of commercial software packages and/or "custom" implementations – designed to support specific functions and developed without a view to a larger enterprise architecture (i.e., closed systems without interoperability, extensibility, etc.). Over 600 Practice Office Management System (POMS) and over 100 Hospital Information System vendors currently supply the healthcare industry with functionally-specific, closed system solutions.

As a result of the reliance on paper-based systems and islands of automation, American healthcare is expensive, bureaucratic, and wasteful. "Twenty-five cents out of every dollar on a hospital bill goes to administrative costs and does not buy any patient care."[3]

7.1.3 Our Vision: Electronic Commerce Services

Information technology can reduce healthcare costs and improve the productivity of physicians and healthcare institutions. Community Health Information Networks (CHINs), as well as Regional, State, and National Health Information

[3] 1993 U.S. Health Security Act, chapter 1.

Networks (for example, in Wisconsin [57]) are all being postulated to address the information requirements of the new virtual healthcare enterprises.

The Healthcare Open Systems and Trials (HOST) Program is a national, industry-based effort to accelerate the deployment of open, interoperable healthcare information systems. HOST is a broad-based partnership of many businesses serving the healthcare community and all stake holders in the healthcare delivery system, e.g., healthcare provider organizations, vendors and suppliers, and information system developers.

General Electric is an active member of HOST and is engaged in formulating and developing open systems healthcare informatics solutions. Our initial goal is to build tools enabling *Electronic Commerce Services (ECS):* "electronic communication among enterprises, including customers, suppliers, business partners, government organizations, and financial institutions."[4] Our tools will help bring ECS to the healthcare industry within the context of the integrated delivery system. Our Electronic Commerce Services vision is to integrate, via open-systems-based networks, complex healthcare enterprises consisting of geographically disparate physicians, hospitals, suppliers, payers, employers, etc., to facilitate the exchange of information.

7.1.4 Potential Benefit

Studies by the Health Care Financing Administration (HCFA) and the Workgroup on Electronic Data Interchange (WEDI) suggest that billions of dollars in administrative costs can be saved in the healthcare arena through the implementation of ECS. If the healthcare industry were to adopt standardized electronic clinical, patient, administrative, insurance and financial transactions, the nation's annual healthcare expenditures could be cut by up to 20 percent. The healthcare industry endorses ECS. Ambitious goals have been set for ECS implementation among the several million potential participants (providers, payers, employers, suppliers, etc.). WEDI recommends that all providers, payers and employers implement four "core" transactions - claim, remittance advice and payment, eligibility, and enrollment - by the end of 1996 and seven additional transactions by the year 2000. HCFA mandates "paperless" Medicare administration by all of HCFA's carriers, intermediaries, and providers by the year 2000.

7.1.5 Structure of This Chapter

We shall amplify on each component of our vision in the remainder of our chapter. We first describe the HOST consortium's structure and objectives for more effective healthcare enterprises, and how electronic commerce is key to realizing these objectives. We then define our team's main technical objectives within HOST: effortless installation for new electronic commerce partners, and tools for automated workflow. We describe our goals for what must be included in

[4] As defined by the Gartner Group.

a workflow system, including an analysis of how currently available workflow products do not meet all of our goals, in particular the need to track the time resources used by important healthcare processes. Finally, we show how a temporal reasoning system can facilitate automated workflow, using our temporal reasoner Tachyon to model and track an example of clinical process flow.

Example Clinical Scenario

We introduce a hypothetical scenario to illustrate several points made in the rest of the chapter. This scenario involves a clinical encounter in a hospital emergency room. This example *within* the hospital enterprise addresses many of the technical workflow challenges to be faced in building electronic commerce *across multiple* enterprises, say in a multi-hospital integrated delivery system.

When a patient enters a hospital emergency room, a variety of actions may occur based on the patient's condition, but there is some commonality across encounters. Let's presume the patient has a minor but not life-threatening pain, such as nose-bleed, chest pain, intestinal pain, or minor limb damage.[5] The patient must be evaluated upon arrival by nurses in "triage" as to how to proceed, while a companion of the patient registers with an emergency room administrator to give patient demographics, billing information, and a brief description of the emergency. Within the triage, the nurse takes the patient history, treats pressing problems, and takes a few preliminary tests - temperature, blood pressure, etc. A resident might also join in this preliminary evaluation.

Several scenarios might occur at this point. The patient might merely need to wait briefly, be re-examined, and be sent home with a prescription (that may be sent to the hospital pharmacy and filled). The patient might be sent for further tests, possibly including X-rays, blood tests, urinalysis, etc. If further tests are taken, a decision must be made as to whether to admit the patient, conduct further tests, or discharge the patient. When the patient is discharged, a billing process among the patient, the hospital, and the patient's insurance provider is begun.

7.2 Our Electronic Commerce Agenda

7.2.1 HOST and Healthcare Information Infrastructure Technology

The Healthcare Open Systems and Trials (HOST) Program is a national, industry-based effort to accelerate the deployment of open, interoperable healthcare information systems. HOST will address the many needs of the emerging community-wide healthcare delivery networks throughout the nation by offering solutions to the problems caused by the proliferation of closed system automation. Fundamental HOST activities include the *Open Systems Laboratory* (OSL) and the

[5] We emphasize the minor patient complaint because we envision different automated workflow templates (see secion 7.3.6) for different patient conditions.

Trial Sites Program. The OSL is a network of laboratories supporting prototype experiments that test systems prior to deployment at "live" sites. The Trial Sites Program is intended to facilitate partnering of industry leaders, advance enterprise-wide information technology and electronic commerce, and address evolving healthcare delivery systems. The Trial Sites program will implement several multi-year, community-wide integration trials. Health information networks and enabling technologies will be established to test and validate emerging technologies and to demonstrate the potential benefits of widespread network deployment.

HOST recently received a major award from the U.S. Department of Commerce. The award of approximately 16 million dollars over three years is the largest awarded under the National Institute of Standards and Technology (NIST) Advanced Technology Program (ATP) competition under the Information Infrastructure for Healthcare focused technology area.

The HOST-sponsored Healthcare Information Infrastructure Technology (HIIT) program is the largest award recipient from 16 projects approved for funding from more than 50 applicants. The HIIT program is an innovative, industry-led initiative involving healthcare and technology experts. The following companies represent the technical leadership for the HIIT program: General Electric (GE), Coleman Research Corporation (CRC), Microelectronics and Computer Technology Corporation (MCC), and TransQuick. Other key participants include small businesses, telecommunication companies, inner-city hospitals, government alliances, universities and prestigious medical centers. The South Carolina Research Authority (SCRA), a leader in consortium management, will be the program facilitator.

HIIT's objective is to develop infrastructure tools that will accelerate the adoption of open systems and enable the development of emergent community health systems. The strategy for developing these tools revolves around the successful interaction among these four infrastructure technology project areas:

- Healthcare Electronic Commerce Services, led by GE
- Enabling Distributed, Rural, and Remote Diagnostics, led by CRC
- Healthcare Enterprise Information Modeling, led by MCC
- Medical Knowledge Bases and Medical Data Capture, led by TransQuick

These four project areas and HOST's Open Systems Laboratory comprise an innovative "hub and spoke" model. The model incorporates OSL as a central hub that supplies common services during research and development as well as later in the life cycle, and provides a vehicle to spur commercialization. The spokes consist of the teams working in each project area.

Our particular spoke of HIIT consists of the following members:

- GE Information Services
- GE Corporate Research and Development

- The Liberty Medical Group, in Baltimore, MD, and
- The Statewide Healthcare Information Network (SHINE), West Virginia

Together this team will implement a representative ECS network in two separate geographic areas, supporting representative subsets of two separate healthcare enterprises. We will work closely together throughout all phases of the project, from requirements analyses through to rapid prototyping, refinement, and evaluations.

7.2.2 Challenges to Electronic Commerce

Technological and financial obstacles stand in the way of achieving our goals of Electronic Commerce Services for the healthcare industry. Experience gained by ECS Value-Added Networks (including GE Information Services) dealing with several industries over the last decade indicates that three major barriers must be overcome in order to realize the potential of Electronic Commerce Services:

- Cost and time required for start-up, i.e., bringing an entity on-line into a virtual enterprise.
- Cost and time required to maintain entities and processes on a virtual enterprise.
- Automation of workflow processes, i.e., moving the right data to the right place at the right time.

We are engaged in two activities to realize our vision and overcome the traditional barriers to implementing ECS: "Effortless" ECS Implementation and Automated Workflow for Virtual Enterprises.

1. *"Effortless" ECS Implementation*: In order to dramatically reduce the cost and time associated with ECS start-up and entity/process maintenance, a tool is needed to assess the functional and connectivity requirements of an entity's coming on-line, and to perform and maintain an ECS installation automatically. Our goal is to reduce the cost and time required to start up a PC-based small business (i.e., a private clinical practice) as a new trading partner by at least an order of magnitude.

   Our spoke of the HIIT project will work together to quickly define the set of requirements on which to base the initial Effortless ECS Implementation prototype. The prototype will be installed at user sites, tested, and continually evaluated. After each evaluation, we will redefine requirements, and upgrade the prototype. In order to prevent the possibility of re-inventing existing capabilities, we will evaluate, and where feasible, utilize, commercial software. We will finally conduct a trial to evaluate the Effortless ECS Implementation prototype in use under realistic day-to-day conditions.

2. *Automated Workflow for Virtual Enterprises*: Our second project is developing tools to capture business process workflow models, to evaluate these models on both simulated and actual data, and to automatically generate scripts for relevant resources in a process. This will enable us to take full advantage of ECS and enable complex processes to be carried out across the virtual enterprise. In Section 7.3 we further describe our goals for workflow tools and analyze current commercial workflow systems.

MCC, a HIIT project spoke leader, will develop tools for representing and enforcing the relevant transactional behavior within health care workflows. This behavior includes maintaining consistency when partially completed workflows must be cancelled and all updated state retracted. The Carnot project at MCC [68], the METEOR project[38] at Bellcore, and work in transactional workflows at several sites [64] have all made strides in this area.

7.2.3 Transactions in a Virtual Health Care Enterprise

We have identified several categories of transactions related to patient care that may benefit from electronic commerce. We list them by type of information. Depending on the content, the transactions may be among some combination of patients, clinicians, payers, and administrators.

- *Procurement:* these are for managing the suppliers and inventories of the healthcare institutions; included are clinical supplies, equipment purchases, and quality control.

- *Clinical:* these include laboratory results, patient history from primary providers, radiology reports, discharge summaries, and other notes that may eventually belong in the patient's multiple charts.

- *Administrative:* these include patient demographics, employer and occupation, consent forms, hospital room and bed scheduling, and secondary payers.

- *Financial:* in addition to the internal accounting of each institution, these include all insurance matters, such as enrollment in health plans, claim encounters, remittance advice, payments, referrals, and approved referral lists.

- *Analytical:* these include matters for monitoring an enterprise's performance, including utilization review, outcomes studies, status of claims with corrections, plan performance analysis, and medical records tracking.

The emergency room example of section 7.1.5 touches upon each category of electronic commerce. Relevant clinical transactions include sending test results across different hospital laboratories and departments, and acquiring the patient's medical records, either from within the hospital or from a primary provider at another site. Administrative transactions might take place as a result of patient registration, admission to the hospital, or scheduling for surgery. Financial transactions include billing for all tests done and services rendered, and in the claims process between the hospital and payers. Analytical transactions are relevant where hospital administrators monitor the use of emergency room and other hospital resources, including time spent in various tasks. Finally, should particular supplies run low or equipment malfunction during an emergency room encounter, procurement transactions might be automatically generated.

7.3 Automated Workflow

7.3.1 Definitions and Objectives

We borrow a definition of *workflow:* a process that automates the flow of documents and related information through the business process [1]. Workflow management includes the sequencing, initiating, monitoring and control of tasks and data. Workflow automation seeks to manage complex, interrelated tasks and the information they utilize and generate. Any business process that is repetitive and requires documents and data to move through the enterprise, real or virtual, is a candidate for the application of workflow. In addition, any business process that requires the exchange and translation of data among different applications and users is a candidate for workflow. Workflow often encompasses tools that support group collaboration on tasks (*groupware*) in addition to routing and tracking. However, we focus largely on those aspects of workflow that address the latter concerns.

Workflow tools should be evaluated with respect to the following capabilities, largely lacking in custom applications and current workflow offerings:

- Simple to use workflow specification tools for businesses to create their own process applications, eliminating the need for custom applications and their associated development time; graphical and script languages are likely to be appropriate;

- Use of organizational roles, rather than specific individual or application addresses as part of the addressing scheme;

- Proper security mechanisms so that only authorized individuals have access to sensitive clinical and financial data;

- Ability to define general business processes using *templates* which may subsequently be made specific by supplying dates, data, specific individuals or roles as participants in the process to be executed;

- Monitoring the status of particular workflows to report the status of the process to the participants, both prior and future;

- Linking of different documents in the context of the process; that is, a particular claim is related to a particular remittance is related to a particular lab report. One might term this linkage as a "case." Such cases must be linked even when temporary loss of control of the document has occurred such as when a task is performed on a local desktop or on a different VAN and the results are subsequently picked up by the workflow;

- Routing of structured documents through the enterprise, using wide-area network (WAN) in addition to the usual LAN connectivity;

- Hierarchies of workflow so that a high level business process may be defined and partitioned into subflows;

- Interfacing with multiple applications that perform the business process tasks; such interoperability is crucial in order to accommodate legacy systems that exist on different platforms;

- Prioritization and load balancing of tasks for workflow participants;

- Incorporation of temporal constraints so that processes can be scheduled and monitored; such monitoring allows monitoring and reporting on the timeliness of the business process and adjusting of the workflow to accommodate delays. Temporal aspects are generally lacking in current workflow offerings.

7.3.2 Workflow in Emergency Room Example

We have mentioned in section 7.2.3 that our emergency room example may require electronic commerce for all transaction types related to patient care. In that context, any benefit of automated workflow tools to healthcare transactions should streamline the emergency room encounter. We also emphasize that while workflow tools may benefit transactions within a particular hospital, these tools can benefit even moreso the multiple environments of an integrated delivery system

Focusing on the clinical transactions of this emergency room encounter, several technical challenges exist in building valuable workflow tools. The relevant patient history may need to come from a primary provider, which must be electronically linked to a hospital. The several patient tests may be reported from different laboratories at different times, yet all must appear together in an integrated patient hospital electronic record. Radiology reports in particular present challenges of integrating images, other graphics, text, and possibly voice annotations; these multiple media must be integrated, transmitted, and displayed effectively. Clinicians reading these lab results are busy with other patients, so that timely and reliable reporting of lab results are essential. The patient, who may be waiting for much of the emergency room encounter, continually needs status information, including when he or she may leave.

7.3.3 Current Commercial Workflow Tools

The list of vendors offering workflow tools and applications is long. Consensus among them as to the features and functions is short. Initially workflow products focused on document-imaging systems, for cataloging and tracking electronic images of paper documents. Today the thinking has shifted to structure and text-based information. Fuller reviews may be found in [37] and [29]. In our brief review we borrow the distinction (made in [37]) between *low-end* and *high-end* based upon the extent of routing possible and the breadth of the enterprise scalability.

Toward the *low-end* are packages such as ActionWorkflow Manager (Action Technologies, Inc.), BeyondMail (Banyan Systems Inc.), FormFlow (Delrina Corp.), Lotus Notes (Lotus Development Corp.) and WorkMan (Reach Software Corp.). Users or at least application developers are able to build workflow applications, often using a graphical user interface (GUI). They vary in their ease-of-use, tracking capabilities, and the ability to handle dynamic workflows, those which must be changed in process. Shortcomings generally include reliance on a central data base to track workflow status, reliance on a single mail engine and lack of the ability to analyze and test a workflow description. Platform dependence is also an issue, as is the strong dependence on e-mail for moving the documents. Each demonstrates strengths that allow much of the workflow task to be accomplished. However, none of them handle complex, dynamic workflow.

High-end products address workflows demanding flexibility of routing, including dynamic workflows with complex conditional routing, involving unpredictable applications. The best high-end products attempt to balance off-the-shelf capabilities with customizable functionality. Object-oriented terms and techniques appear in the product descriptions. Also, at the high-end are those products that can be used by a large distributed enterprise whereas many of the low-end operate only within a local-area network (LAN). High-end products tend to require UNIX servers, although PC-based products are appearing. Vendors include Xerox (InConcert), FileNet (Workflow), IBM (FlowMark) and TASC (TASC-Flow). These products need to be evaluated with the healthcare virtual enterprise in mind. As virtual enterprises are formed, reformed and disbanded, there is a requirement for dynamic workflows that can integrate with existing distributed (unpredictable) legacy applications operating in the participant's environment.

7.3.4 Workflow Applications to Clinical Health Care

Several recent projects have applied workflow to model clinical transactions in healthcare. The breadth of approaches here is similar to that of applied workflow research in other disciplines. Pisanelli et al. have worked on integrating and managing multimedia patient folders for radiology departments [61], and have not yet focused on routing these folders within a larger clinical environment.

Several researchers have applied state-based models to clinical workflow scenarios. Srinivasan et al. [28] have developed workflow models for tracking medical charts using Parameterized Petri Nets (PPN). In the PPN, tokens represent medical records, states represent locations the records may be found (admitting, nurses station, records deptartment, etc.) and transitions represent processes that relocate the records (patient signing in, doctor ordering tests or treatments, etc.). The PPN is simulated, with time delays built in between transitions, to analyze the movement of multiple charts throughout a hospital. The simulations are useful for considering different record management strategies. Gangopadhyay and Wu have developed models with checkpoint states for clinical processes [25], such as generating and filling prescriptions. Kuhn et al's activity templates [7] are models of processes whose resources are distributed throughout a clinical information system. Each of these approaches has investigated the advanced representation requirements for a particular aspect of internal hospital workflow; we seek to do similar analyses on a virtual enterprise-wide scale.

7.3.5 Role for Temporal Reasoning

An explicit temporal reasoning system can help in tracking particular tasks in an actual process, in measuring whether a process runs efficiently over time, and in re-desigining models of the processes. For each contribution listed below, we describe what questions can be answered, and refer to the emergency room encounter.

- *Tracking individual tasks.* By answering the question, "How long will a particular task take?" a temporal reasoner can help individuals in a process better manage their time. For example, a physician who sent a patient for blood tests would like to know how soon to expect the results. Similarly, a patient waiting in the emergency room lounge may wish some estimate of when she can expect to go home.

- *Measuring overall process efficiency.* By answering questions like "Over the past week, how much time has a department spent on these particular tasks?" a temporal reasoner helps an administrator or planner judge the efficiency of business processes. For example, a hospital administrator can track if patient registration at the emergency has been taking unusually long, and try to find and fix the root of any problem.

- *Improving scheduling.* By answering "How many temporally overlapping processes are using the same resources?" a temporal reasoner brings two main benefits. Should a workflow simulation show that many concurrent tasks require the same resources, a planner can better schedule the processes, and adjust the corresponding workflow models, so that resources are better utilized. In the emergency room, the problem may be too many patients scheduled at once for X-rays so that a queue results at the radiology department. The workflow model can be adjusted to allow the X-rays to be staggered, and other information gathered earlier in some patients.

- *Managing inventory and procurement.* Answering the immediately preceeding question also assists managers of inventory and purchasing. If genuine resource conflicts exist and cannot be resolved by modifying the process, then new equipment may need to be purchased or new staff hired. Conversely, if resources are being underutilized, equipment or staff may be expendable.

Explicit temporal reasoning tools are not currently available in automated workflow tools. We suspect there are two main reasons: resource requirements, and a misconception about utility. As we shall describe, proper management of the temporal resources of a process requires tools for representing the expected temporal durations of tasks, and the temporal constraints across different tasks. A sophisticated interface and reasoner, integrated with the rest of the workflow system, is required to encode and repeatedly update these constraints. These valuable components require development time and computational resources rarely found in current commercial systems.

Explicit tracking of time resources can amplify the time and cost savings found by electronic commerce, and the associated business process re-engineering. Temporal reasoning can help insure that electronic transactions occur in a timely manner, and can provide valuable information to assist in the cycle of process re-engineering. We caution against complacent thinking mere automation of commerce insures sufficient process improvement.

7.3.6 Preliminary Workflow Architecture

The basis of our workflow architecture is a language for representating classes of workflows appropriate to some particular type of process. We call each class a *workflow template*. Each workflow template consists of a set of interrelated task classes, linked in several dimensions. Tasks within the same workflow may be related in their temporal durations, they may share personnel, they may share equipment or space resources.

The workflow template language will draw upon specialization hierarchies of trading partners, resources, and documents. We plan to use object-oriented modelling techniques. For example, the class of trading partners *Blue Cross Insurer* is a leaf on a specialization branch:

```
Financial partner -> insurer -> medical insurer -> Blue Cross insurer
```

An *instance* of the leaf node might be the particular insurer *Blue Cross of Maryland.*

The task classes within a workflow template will be selected from another taxonomic hierarchy, linked by specialization and decomposition, much in the spirit of the organizational workflow models of Malone et al. [39]. Each task in the hierarchy is defined in part by role fillers coming from the trading partner, resource, and document hierarchies. For example, the task class representing a transmission of ANSI-standard 837 EDI health claims is defined thusly:

```
ANSI-837 transmission
subclass of Claims Transaction
```

```
Sender role is Medical Provider
Receiver Role is Medical Payer
Document Role is ANSI-837-EDI Document
```

Each task class description must include the required resources, including personnel, equipment, space, and time. Personnel resources can be represented not only by identifying particular people but also by describing personnel by *functional roles.* For the time resources, each task class within a workflow template is associated with a *temporal interval*, representing the duration in time of the task. The temporal interval is uncertain in its begin times, end times, and duration.

Workflow templates are instantiated for actual processes; part of the instantiation is making specific the actual resources being used for each task. Templates are instantiated partially, with task instances added incrementally as decisions are made within a process.

7.4 Temporal Reasoning for Workflow

In this section we will discuss some of the key requirements that a temporal reasoning system must support to ensure a powerful and flexible capability for workflow. Many of these are discussed in the context of Tachyon, a prototype software tool for constraint-based temporal reasoning that we are building at GE Corporate Research and Development (GE CR&D) as part of the ARPA/Rome Laboratory Planning Initiative (ARPI) [20]. Much of what we present here can be applied regardless of the tools used for temporal reasoning support for workflow; we have, however, tried to address in Tachyon many of the issues that arise in workflow modeling and reasoning. As a result, this tool and its associated algorithms provide an appropriate framework for discussion.

7.4.1 Tachyon

Temporal reasoning problems arise in numerous computer applications. In addition to the workflow application area that is the focus of this chapter, temporal reasoning is important in such areas as databases, simulators, expert systems, and industrial scheduling and planning systems (minimizing assembly line slack time, projecting critical steps in a deployment plan to insure proper interaction between them, etc.). All these need to manipulate temporal information to model the world. Although some ability to model and manipulate such information has been built into some existing software systems, it has usually been minimal, making simplifying assumptions and failing to capture the richness and complexity that accompany full integration of temporal representations. This is especially true when incompleteness of information, non-instantaneous events, complex temporal relationships, or uncertainty pervade the application domain.

We at GE CR&D have been involved in research and development in temporal reasoning for the past several years, focusing on developing a powerful approach to temporal reasoning that has the flexibility to be useful in a diverse set of application areas. In particular, we have developed Tachyon, a prototype software tool for constraint-based temporal reasoning being built as part of the ARPA/Rome Laboratory Planning Initiative (ARPI).

One of the key reasons we began developing Tachyon was as a research vehicle to explore new techniques for dealing with the inherent complexity of temporal reasoning and scheduling. We have recognized it's applicability to a number of problems of both military and commercial interest, and have simultaneously sought opportunities to explore the appropriateness of using Tachyon in a diverse set of applications. Thus far we have applied Tachyon successfully in a number of problem areas of both military and commercial importance (see, for instance, [76]). These include manufacturing scheduling problems, force expansion, plan recognition tasks(where Tachyon was used to validate temporal sequencing of events as an aid in formulating plan hypotheses), plan generation and monitoring, and retrieval and situation refinement in a prototype spatio-temporal data management system [75].

There are several features of Tachyon that will be useful in applying it to workflow problems. These include its ability to:

- deal with uncertainty regarding the exact time and duration of occurrence of events, e.g., the X-ray will occur sometime in the morning, and patient registration takes between 5 and 20 minutes;
- express both qualitative and quantitative constraints between events, e.g., X is before or meets Y, and X ends between 15 and 20 days before Y starts;
- express parameterized qualitative constraints between events, e.g., X is before Y by at most 6 days,
- promote ease of use via graphical input and display capabilities,
- run as a subprocess in other applications as well as stand-alone,
- utilize techniques that will remain effective even in very large application domains,
- cope effectively with the intractability associated with disjoint constraints.

In what follows below, we describe some specific aspects of Tachyon's representation, reasoning capabilities, and implementation.

Representation

A graph-based temporal constraint network (TCN) paradigm, which Tachyon exemplifies, meets several of these desiderata well. A constraint network is a graph in which nodes correspond to variables and edges constrain the values the associated variables can be assigned. Assigning values to the variables is an instantiation. An instantiation satisfies a constraint if the variable assignments do not violate the constraint. A graph instantiation is consistent if it satisfies all the constraints of the network.

There are several advantages to using TCNs to represent temporal relationships, including easy visualization through graphical representation and the ability (in some circumstances) to use linear programming techniques to propagate information throughout the network quickly. Temporal constraint networks typically use quantitative values to express the allowable relationships between events. In our work we have also conformed to this, using a "point-based" representation of time. The other prominent representational paradigm for time is found in James Allen's interval calculus. Allen [2] developed a set of qualitative linguistic values for describing relationships between events. Qualitative constraints allow one to specify relationships between events using linguistic descriptions, without numeric bounding. For instance, we may want to express abstract temporal ordering on a medical supplier's delivery route by saying that hospital A is visited before hospital B, without specifying when either delivery is made or numerically constraining the time between the two deliveries. Deviation from that sequence should be identified as causing temporal inconsistency. A qualitative network is inconsistent when there exists an unresolvable conflict between instantiated variables and their constraints. In the above example, specifying A before B, but giving B earlier times than A results in inconsistency.

before	←x→ ←y→	after	←x→ ←y→
meets	←—x⊣ ⊢y—→	metby	⊢x—→ ←—y⊣
overlaps	←—x—→ ←—y—→	overlappedby	←—x—→ ←—y—→
starts	⊢x→ ⊢y—→	startedby	⊢x—→ ⊢y→
during	←x→ ←—y—→	contains	←—x—→ ←y→
finishes	←x⊣ ←—y⊣	finishedby	←—x⊣ ←y⊣
equals	⊢x⊣ ⊢y⊣		

Table 7.1: **Allen Relations** The relation x -(e.g., before)- y is illustrated by the relative positions of the intervals in this table. Simultaneous starts and finishes are indicated by vertical end-brackets (⊢), while the angular end-brackets (←) indicate otherwise. Line length represents relative duration of the events.

Although a point-based representation is to be preferred for many of the temporal reasoning tasks we face, it is often convenient to allow relationships to be expressed using qualitative values. The Tachyon model supports constraint specification using either quantitative or qualitative representation. This also allows some expansion in expressiveness of qualitative relationships, e.g., parameterized qualitative constraints such as at least 2 hours before, with no performance penalty.

Tachyon represents events using 6-tuples to help capture uncertainty in event occurrence and duration. The 6-tuple associated with each node represents an event's earliest and latest possible start times, earliest and latest possible finish times, minimum and maximum possible durations. We also extend expression of constraints to allow both quantitative and qualitative relationships between events. To represent the same information in many other models an event must artificially be divided into a start event and a finish event, with a constraint between the two indicating duration. The 6-tuple representation allows a single node to map to an entire real-world event, accounting for both duration and uncertainty. The added event expressiveness demands similar expansion of the constraint model. Tachyon networks use a point based representation with numerical distances between events. Such quantitative constraints place numerical bounds on the temporal relationship between two events. For example, we should be able to express the constraint that a scan can't be started on a given x-ray machine until some interval is allowed for changeover from the previous scan. This interval is known (at least within some bounds) and any deviation from it should be found to be inconsistent. Qualitative constraints are expressed using epsilon, the smallest distance possible, and infinity, the largest. For example, the qualitative relation before is interpreted as "There is a non-zero, positive distance between Event 1 and Event 2." Thus, we can say the distance between Event 1 and Event 2 is at least epsilon, at most infinity.

In Tachyon, one can also expand on Allen's linguistic relationships by adding parameters to some of the relations. For instance, instead of simply saying you can't eat before a blood test, you might say that you can't eat within 12 hours prior to a blood test. Parameterization is an option for the qualitative relations before, overlaps, overlapped by, and after. Each of these is given the ability to take on two parameters, representing the minimum and maximum distance to which they refer. One must exercise care in introducing such parameterized qualitative relationships as they can introduce intractability. Edge constraints are expressed internally by an 8-tuple in Tachyon. The 8-tuple constraint between event nodes 1 and 2 represents the minimum and maximum time between start1 and start2, minimum and maximum time between start1 and finish2, minimum and maximum time between finish1 and start2, minimum and maximum time between finish1 and finish2.

Reasoning

Tractable Cases Tachyon uses a modification of the Bellman-Ford shortest-path algorithm to propagate information and tighten the bounds of variables in the graph. This is sufficient for graphs that consist solely of convex constraints[6]

[6] A constraint between two events X and Y is *convex* if and only if the possible durations of X with respect to Y forms a continuous (i.e. not disjoint) region on the time line.

and differs from Dechter et. al., who use the Floyd-Warshall algorithm. Descriptions of these can be found in [43]. Both algorithms have $O(n^3)$ time complexity, where n is the number of nodes. In the testing we have done, the Bellman-Ford algorithm provided a substantial performance increase over the Floyd-Warshall algorithm, especially when the corresponding graphs are fairly sparse. Based partially on this testing, we are confident that Tachyon is considerably more efficient than other approaches, despite its expressive model.

Nonconvex Constraints Sometimes we must specify constraints that are problematic in that they introduce intractability to the reasoning process. Such constraints are called nonconvex or disjoint, and occur in many practical planning and scheduling applications. Unfortunately, introducing them may greatly increase the complexity of processing the network. For example, consider a single x-ray machine, and two patients needing x-rays; they cannot use the machine simultaneously. The constraint we need to state is "Patient 1 will use the machine (before or after) patient 2." Such disjoint constraints, which require performance of multiple tasks on a single vehicle/tool/machine without precedence constraints between the competing tasks, arise frequently in planning and scheduling domains. Tachyon currently provides capability for specifying nonconvex constraints, and some capability for solving such sets. One of the formidable obstacles we must overcome (or at least minimize) to provide such capabilities for large systems is that of the inherent computational intractability of finding consistent solutions to large, complex networks of constraints that arise in practice. (Most of these problems take exponential time to solve under the commonly believed assumption about deterministic computation that P $\neq$ NP.)

Interface

Tachyon can be used as an embedded temporal reasoning system and as a stand-alone file-driven system. It also has a graphical user interface (GUI), shown in figure 7.1.

This graphical editor allows loading and saving of temporal data files that are compatible with the batch mode version. Thus, one can use Tachyon to test consistency of a network, fine tune it, or test it in "What if..." scenarios as desired, then save the network in a file the batch-mode system can use. The testing of alternate scenarios fits within our project goals of building a workflow simulator (see section 7.2.2).

The interface itself is a modeless direct-manipulation editor for the graphical representation of the underlying network. Nodes and edges are tied to pop-up menus which allow modification and entry of the associated values in the data base. A menu scheme that enforces convexity on the constraint is used when selecting Allen relations. The canvas on which the graph appears can be panned and sized as needed. Nodes and edges can be added, moved, deleted, etc. as desired.

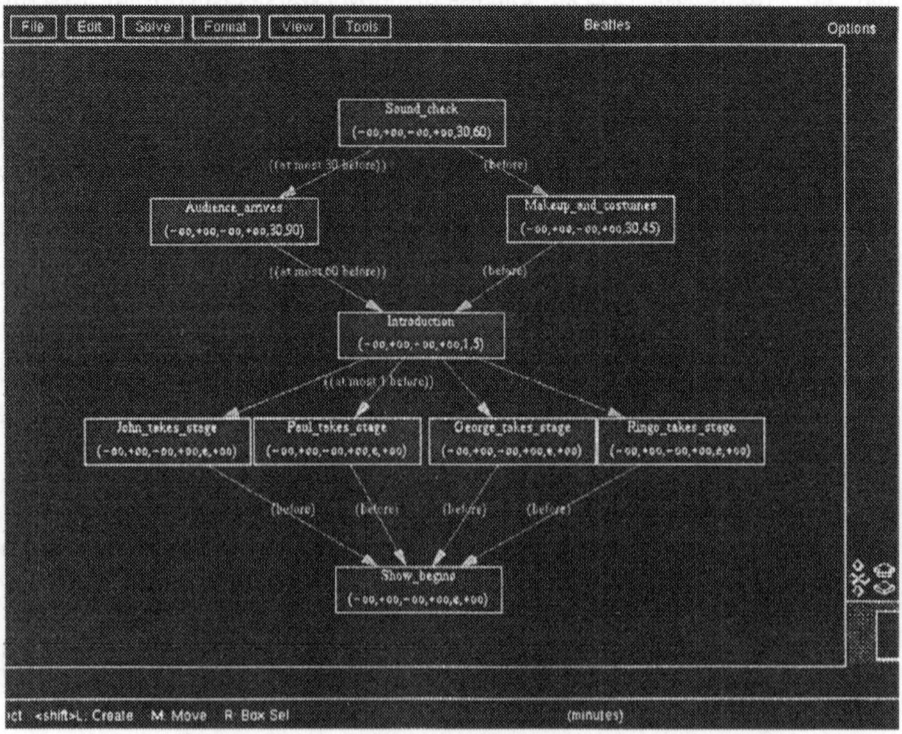

Figure 7.1 A simple example of Tachyon's use.

7.4.2 Example Temporal Workflow Models

In this section we introduce a temporal workflow model corresponding to our emergency room example of section 7.1.5, to demonstrate how temporal reasoning might play a role in workflow for medical information systems.

Temporal Template

In Figure 7.2 we present a *temporal template* of a set of events associated with a typical patient's course of treatment upon arriving at an emergency room. Note that the times associated with each of the events are uninstantiated, but we are still able to capture information about the range of durations of the events, and the constraints that exist between events. All numerically encoded durations are expressed in minutes. Thus, for example, the duration of the `Triage` task is from ten minutes to sixty minutes.

Note that the temporal constraints linking events cover a broad range of qualitative temporal interval relationships. For example, four temporal relations are possible between the broader task **Triage** and the subtask **Prelim Tests**: equals, finished by, started by, or contains.

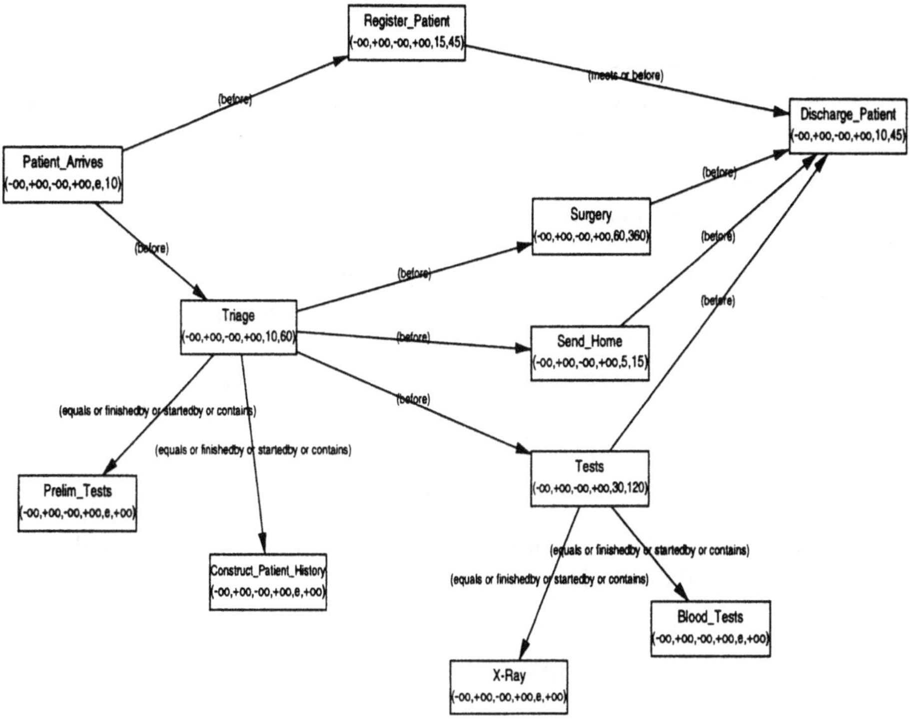

Figure 7.2: A Tachyon network showing a temporal template for an emergency room encounter.

Partial Temporal Instance

In Figure 7.3 we have instantiated the template by adding the arrival time for a particular patient and propagating this new information through the constraint network. Note, for instance, that we can begin to make deductions about when the patient may be available to be scheduled for tests.

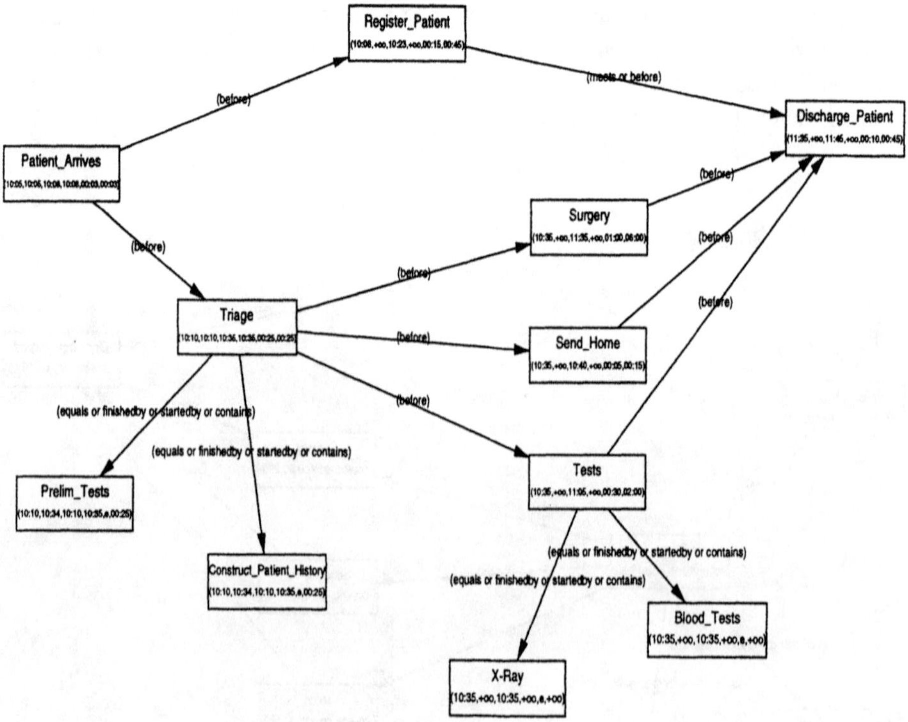

Figure 7.3: The emergency room example, with partial instantiation and propagation of temporal constraints.

7.4.3 Tracking Processes

One important workflow objective currently achievable with our temporal reasoner is *tracking* of tasks: querying for ranges on the duration of tasks and ranges of end times of tasks. We illustrate here at first with a simple temporal model for a blood test task, and then within the larger emergency room scenario.

Blood Test Sub-Task

Consider the workflow task `Blood Tests` of the emergency room scenario, illustrated in section 7.4.2. A physician may send a patient for blood tests in a hospital, and the physician later expects to find the laboratory results in the hospital's on-line reporting system. We may represent this process as a series of consecutive phases:

- the patient is in transit from the physician's office to the laboratory
- the patient waits to have blood drawn.
- a technician draws blood from the patient, and sends out the sample for interpretation.
- another technician interprets the lab results
- the results are (perhaps manually) entered into the laboratory reporting database.

Objectives

Throughout a hospital's operation, expectations may be gathered as to the minimum and maximum durations reasonable for each of these five phases. Additionally, guidelines or standards may be established as to time ranges for each step in this process, for improving productivity.

Given that the lab results may be critical for the physician's therapy planning for the patient (as in diabetic ketoacidosis or in the intensive care unit patient), that physician may wish to know, at any time during this process, how much longer (within bounds) until the lab results are available. A hospital administrator may wish to know how often each phase of this process takes longer than expectations or standards. Furthermore, an automated workflow system may wish to send a reminder to an employee if his or her part of the process has taken longer than the expected bounds. Reminders such as these may improve hospital productivity.

Temporal Models for Tracking

Figure 7.4 shows a temporal model of the blood test process in a hospital. The model consists of five intervals, each corresponding to the temporal duration of one of the phases outlined in the previous section. The intervals are connected by "meets" constraints, indicating that the endpoints of consecutive intervals meet. The intervals are annotated with minimum and maximum start times, finish times, and durations. For example, the duration of the "Move Patient To Laboratory" interval is a minimum of 10 minutes and a maximum of 20 minutes. These durations might be standards set by some external source, or might be 99 percent confidence intervals for duration learned from studying timings of past patients.

In practice, this temporal model serves as a template against which each actual patient blood test may be instantiated for monitoring that test's workflow. This template is instantiated in part by anchoring a time in the temporal model to a clock time. We envision electronic means (e.g., a patient ID and codes for each workflow template) of entering times for each patient's starting or completion of each task within a workflow. Thus, when a doctor instructs patient-333 at 2:10 p.m. to go to the lab for tests, the automated workflow system instructs

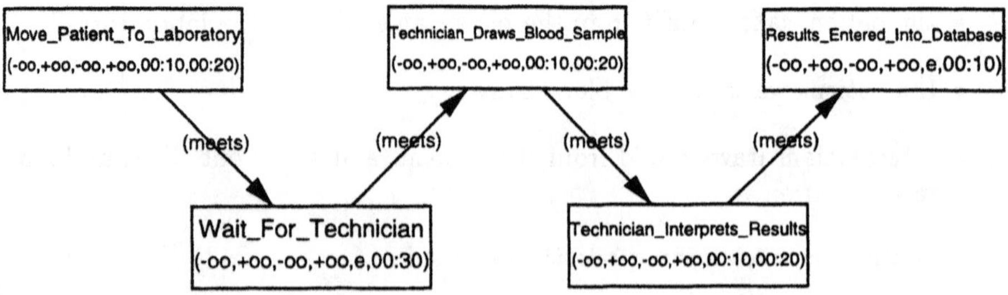

Figure 7.4 Temporal model for blood tests in a hospital.

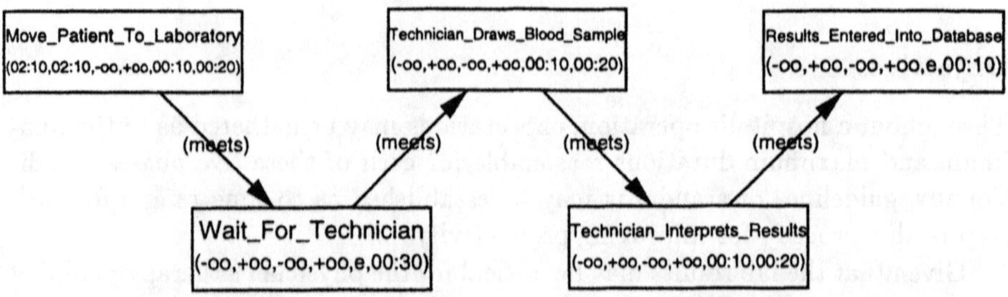

Figure 7.5 Temporal model with start time asserted.

its temporal reasoner that the "Move Patient To Laboratory" interval began at precisely 2:10, as reflected in the updated model shown in Figure 7.5.

Once the temporal workflow template is thus instantiated, a physician may ask the workflow system for bounds on when the lab results should be in the database. The workflow system generates a query for the temporal reasoner, requesting the required interval. Under a temporal constraint network implementation such as Tachyon, this would in turn cause the temporal reasoner to propagate the time values through the network, producing the refined workflow instance shown in Figure 7.6.

The given query is answered by reading the finish time interval of the "Results Entered Into Database" interval, which results in the interval (2:38, 3:50).

Similarly, if a patient has had blood drawn by 2:34 p.m., the temporal database for this workflow can be updated by asserting the finish times on the "Technician Draws Blood Sample" interval and re-propagating the network, as shown in Figure 7.7.

With this updated information the temporal reasoner can return the more refined range of end of the blood test process: (2:44 p.m., 3:04 p.m.).

Using these calculations of when each phase of the instantiated workflow should end, a workflow monitoring system can periodically check if each phase

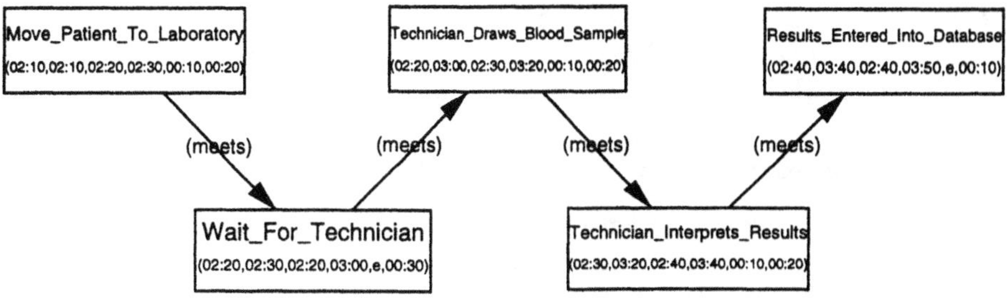

Figure 7.6 Propagated temporal model.

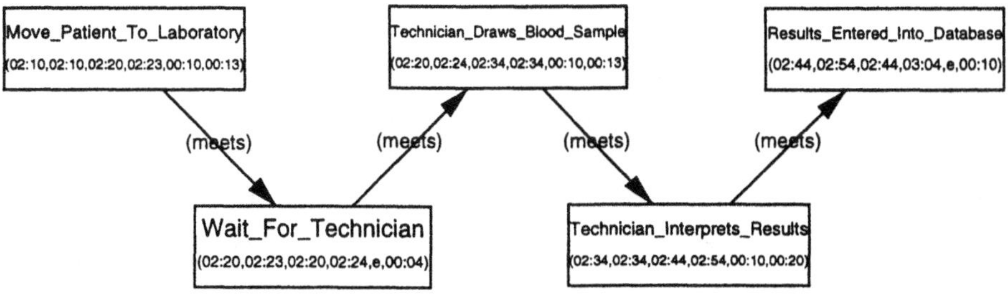

Figure 7.7 Propagated temporal model with additional information.

of the process has been completed before its latest bound. If a phase has not been completed yet it should have, an alarm can be sent to the individual person (or more generally, agent) responsible for that phase.

Overall Emergency Room Task

Coming back to the overall emergency room temporal instance of Figure 7.3, Tachyon can in fact answer these relevant tracking queries:

- *What is the earliest the patient can expect to leave?* The answer is 11:45 p.m.
- *How long was spent gathering patient history for this patient?* The answer is between 0 and 25 minutes.

7.4.4 Extensions to Temporal Reasoner

While Tachyon's capabilities meet a number of key requirements for temporal reasoning for workflow, there are also several areas in which extensions would be quite useful. We outline several of these below.

Hierarchical Specification

We have seen how the temporal aspects of a workflow system can be modeled in terms of temporal constraints applied to the temporal intervals associated with tasks in the workflow. The organization and management of a workflow is typically hierarchical in nature. In such a representation, more complex workflows are decomposed into networks of simpler workflows, which can be subsequently decomposed further, and so on until a suitable level of detail has been achieved. Hierarchical models are more expressive, allowing one to capture the various levels of organization in a workflow, and the dependence relationships that exist at each level. An analyst can choose to examine a high-level, low-detail representation of the system, or particular sub-systems can be examined in a low-level, high-detail manner.

The benefits of hierarchical modeling methods manifest themselves in the modeling and analysis of temporal aspects of a workflow. In its most general form, a hierarchical temporal constraint network consists of a number of levels of tasks, as shown in Figure 7.8. At a given level, sets of tasks can be logically grouped together to define a higher-level task. The relationship of a given task to its component sub-tasks can be expressed as:

> A task is said to have *started* when one or more of its sub-tasks have started. A task is said to have *finished* when all of its sub-tasks are finished.

Of course, *elementary* tasks, which lie at the lowest level of the hierarchy and are not decomposed into sub-tasks, have the standard non-hierarchical temporal semantics, and are treated as simple temporal intervals in the temporal model.

A potentially beneficial operation that can be performed on hierarchically structured temporal networks is a partial propagation of temporal values in localized regions of the hierarchical network. A situation in which such an operation may be useful, for example, would be one in which a workflow's temporal network has been instantiated from the lowest level up to a particular level in the hierarchy. An analyst may want to know the temporal interval of a given task in the next higher level as specified by the instantiated sub-tasks alone, i.e., ignoring any constraints between the high-level task and its siblings at the same level. Performing a local propagation from a given level to a single task in the next higher level would provide potentially useful information on the temporal bounds of the given task, without performing a constraint network propagation on the fully expanded network.

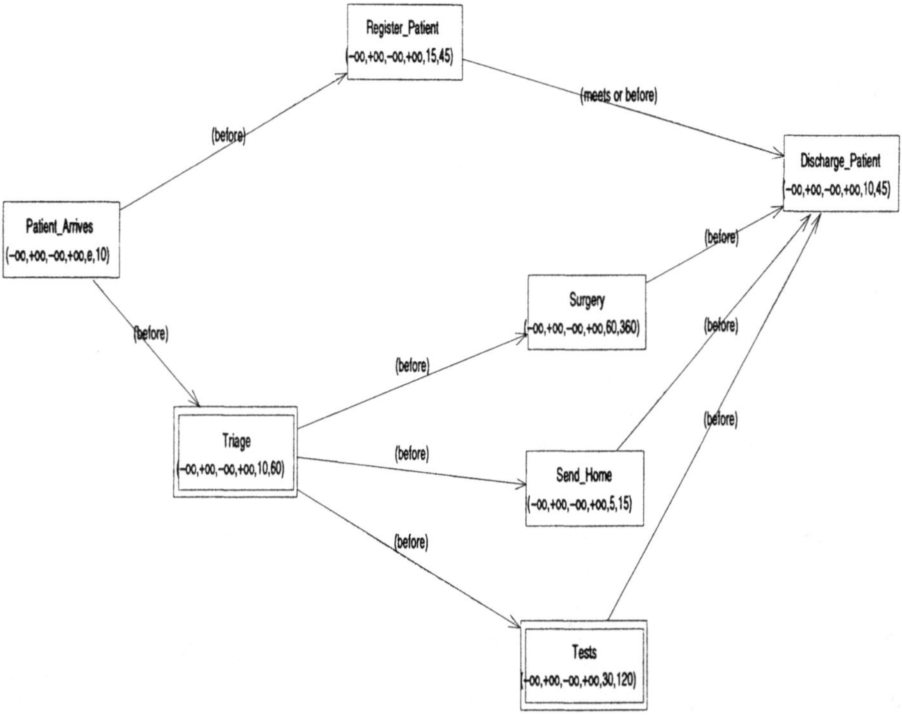

Figure 7.8: The emergency room example, with a hierarchical presentation of the same network as above. Note that the **Triage** and **Test** events have been treated as hierarchical, and their subnetworks have been collapsed.

Integration with Planning, Triggers

In general, temporal reasoning involves reasoning about the temporal interrelationships between events. In some situations we would like to do more; for example, the occurrence of an event might serve as a trigger for a specified action to be invoked. This is a capability that often involves integration of an AI planner with a temporal reasoner. Such situations arise frequently in workflow problems: we may want the system to automatically enable or initiate an action to route a form to a new location based on when a particular event occurred (either at its start or its finish). For example, in a temporal reasoning system such as Tachyon, we can specify that after a patient has been operated upon, a set of actions should be undertaken, perhaps including notifying the scheduling system that the surgical team and the operating room are available, setting a course of post-operative care, updating the billing system, and notifying the doctor treating the patient. The temporal reasoner will provide a means of developing the associated constraint system and will provide reasoning support, but has no means of ensuring that the steps that must be performed to route the results are undertaken. Unlike the hierarchical specification capability discussed above, this is most effectively a layer that is somewhat isolated from the temporal reasoner, acting as a cooperating process. We have experience in developing such coordinated applications through our work in integrating Tachyon with two generative planning systems and with a case-based reasoning system [8].

Flexibility to Allow Lateness

Temporal reasoning systems tend to be inflexible with respect to lateness. Their role in this regard is simply to inform the "user" that there exists a violation of the existing constraints. Some systems, including Tachyon, provide some guidance in determining where the conflict exists. In general, they can do little more, as there is little one can exploit automatically to determine how to fix a violation of the stated constraints. In many applications, including scheduling and workflow, lateness is a regular occurrence. We envision a system in which users can denote the fact that a given task can be allowed to slip beyond its latest specified finish times. This would provide the flexibility necessary for fully exploiting templates to specify temporal aspects of workflow, i.e., the designer of the workflow template could specify that if certain tasks fail to meet their stated latest allowable finish times, they (and perhaps others) can have their latest allowable finish times extended in the particular instance. This allows the designer to specify the desired model without overconstraining the system to the point of brittleness.

Contingent Constraints

One of the important aspects of building temporal workflow models is the ability to represent and reason about exclusive alternative scenarios. Thus we would like to be able to specify within a single model that after examination the patient is either admitted for observation or is discharged (perhaps depending on the outcome of a test), but never both simultaneously. There are several choices with respect to how to implement such a capability. One could expand the temporal model to accommodate such alternatives, or one can add a layer that maintains a library of temporal models, and selects the model that applies based on the outcome of the "test." Each approach has its advantages and disadvantages. The former allows some deduction to take place over the space of "possible worlds," i.e., the space of all possible instantiations of contingent constraints, but such deductive capability is computatonally intractable and thus of limited practical applicability. The latter is computationally tractable, but doesn't provide nearly the deductive power. Thus one would be able to use the former to ask when a a new patient is admitted, whether the patient will be available for surgery between 6:00 and 6:30 regardless of which of a specified alternative set of tests is chosen, but in the latter model, one would only be able to deduce the patient's availability for surgery once the particular test is chosen. This problem is also closely related to the situation described above in which aspects of events serve as triggers for a specified set of actions.

7.5 Conclusions

We have demonstrated through example clinical scenarios, and results with our temporal reasoner Tachyon that temporal reasoning can be a valuable tool for managing and improving the workflow of business processes, particularly in healthcare. We have also identified areas where Tachyon can be extended to provide even more support for automated workflow.

Temporal reasoning is but one key component of our development plans to develop tools for automated workflow in healthcare. Our work will also make use of knowledge acquisition using graphical tools, resource logistics, simulation, and likns to EDI. These various capabilities must fit together within the workflow package.

Although tools for automated workflow tools are but one step in our ultimate vision for electronic commerce for virtual healthcare enterprises, a successfully implemented workflow environment is both a benchmark and a building block in that vision. It is a benchmark in that implemented workflow indicates that basic connectivity has been achieved. It is a building block in that implemented workflow allows an enterprise to monitor and improve its processes continually.

Acknowledgements

D.J. Crane, Dan Roe, and Raj Chopra of G. E. Information Services have guided our vision for this project and offered comments on this chapter. James Comly and Jackie Luciano of G. E. Corporate Research and Development have shared in project activities and discussions. Amit Sheth of the University of Georgia and Douglas B. Fridsma of Stanford University have helped with both principled discussions on workflow and suggestions for technical references.

Chapter 8

The Information Marketplace: Achieving Success in Commercial Applications

Steve Laufmann [1]

8.1 The Information Marketplace

Information is useful for a broad variety of tasks and is increasingly being turned to commercial advantage. As the computing and communication infrastructures for the information marketplace mature, enterprises will most likely evolve in ways that will ultimately emulate those seen in the traditional commercial world - namely, a complex blend of independent providers and consumers, interacting in various ways to provide and consume a broad range of wholesale, retail, and facilitation services.

The work described herein is based on the premise that the basic *foundations* of commerce, including the formulas, functions, and processes of commerce, will not appreciably change even as the coming electronic and information revolution changes the *forms* of commerce. Existing commercial processes evolved over a long period of time, so we assume that they accurately reflect the inherent nature of humans in commercial activities. In essence, these functions succeeded because they work. It is unlikely that changes in the forms taken by these processes will radically affect the basic functions.

Thus, it is important to carefully and deliberately consider *existing* commercial activities in designing and proposing new technologies to support them in the future. We must be diligent to understand and respect existing commercial functions in designing new forms. Even though it is possible that early forms of information commerce may not closely resemble existing commercial activities, it is likely that they will either quickly evolve around the same commercial functionality.

This chapter addresses the needs and desires of commercial service providers for offering commercially viable online services to their customers. This vision for future applications, is based on laboratory experimentation with various technologies for information commerce, together with an understanding of customers

[1] U S WEST Technologies 4001 Discovery Drive, Boulder, CO 80303, Email: laufmann@advtech.uswest.com

and marketing issues, and a vision for future technological foundations and environments. This chapter describes this vision rather than an implemented environment, as only some portions of this vision have been implemented to date. Section 2 presents a simple model of commerce, and discusses the roles and variations in this model. Section 3 notes key observations of the state of commercial activities today. Our vision for the information marketplace is presented in section 4. Section 5 documents the key technological and business challenges facing the developers of the information marketplace. Section 6 presents our three-part approach and its implications, while section 7 briefly introduces the implementations and application prototype. The advantages and disadvantages of this approach are discussed in section 8, and section 9 presents an overview of work remaining to be done in the future. Conclusions are given in section 10.

8.2 Commerce Model

This discussion is based on a simple commerce model, in which information can be the *means* by which commerce occurs and at the same time the *article* of commerce. The boundary between these uses of information is not distinct, and will not be explored in depth here. This model includes three roles, as shown in Figure 1.

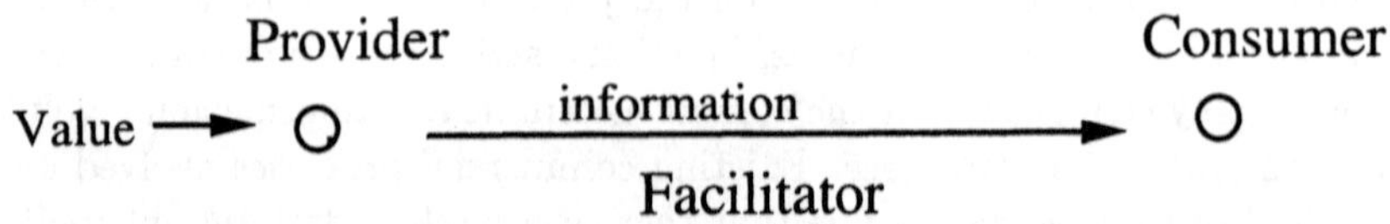

Figure 8.1: Figure 1. A simple model of the roles required in information commerce.

- The *provider* - the information source, which creates something of value which can be bought and sold in the information marketplace. The provider need not offer what would be considered a traditional "information service." Instead, the service may involve some form of problem-solving activity, such as plumbing consultation, landscape architecture, or tax advice. In whatever form, the provider injects value into the overall system.
- The *consumer* - the information sink, which consumes that thing of value. This role may involve browsing, requesting assistance, purchasing informa-

tion, or using various services. In so doing the consumer incurs expenses, and appropriate payment is eventually made to the provider(s).

- The *facilitator* - the provider(s) of the environment, transport channel, and related support services. This role enables providers and consumers to interact efficiently, over distance if necessary, to securely exchange information and services. This may include formatting, transport, staging and presentation, advertising, security services, registration, indexing, and support operations such as billing and payment collection. This role is roughly analogous to the owner of a shopping mall, providing an accessible, comfortable, and secure environment within which sellers and buyers can transact business.

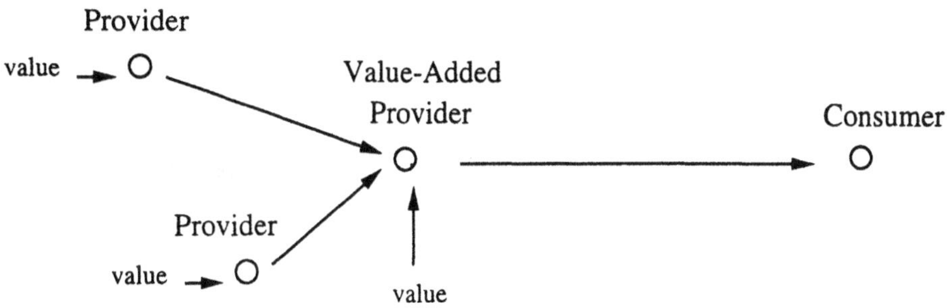

Figure 8.2 Figure 2. An extended model: value-added providers.

Value-added providers (see Figure 2) combine the consumer and provider roles, obtaining "raw" information from various sources (consuming), adding value in the form of additional information or services, and repackaging the results for consumption (providing). In many cases the aggregated, processed, and repackaged information will no longer resemble the "raw" information upon which it is based. For example, an investment service might take raw stock prices from one source, information about Treasury bills from another, and commodity price data from others, then perform a trend analysis, and finally offer buy or sell recommendations. The new service may repackage raw information into a more useful form without requiring consumers to know the location, format, or access mechanisms of the raw information. In using the wholesale services, the final consumer need not worry about the pricing or payment strategies required to gain access to the raw information, since the value-added provider performs these functions and bears the associated costs as a wholesale buyer. The provider that delivers the service to an end consumer assumes the role of retail provider.

Figure 3 shows how services may be bought and sold in different ways in a larger network of services. There are two distinct forms of consumption, each

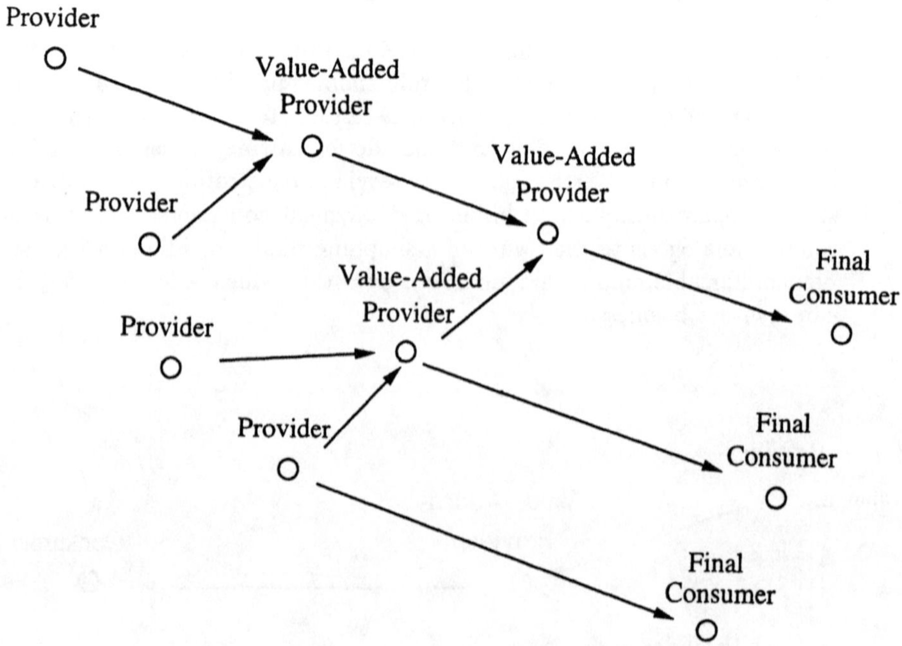

Figure 8.3 Figure 3. The extension of the commerce model.

requiring different tools and techniques. The first is machine-based (i.e., mechanized) access to services, which requires the specification of well-defined service access protocols and languages. The second is human-based access (i.e., manual), and requires platform-independent user interfaces. Providers must choose whether and how to provide these in the creation of their service. This choice will determine how the service is accessed and used. The access tools are described in sections 6.2 and 6.3.
Wholesale services may be offered to consumers in two fundamentally different forms. In the first, raw information is fully consumed in the provision of the value-added service. The value provided by the wholesale service is "swallowed up" by the value-added provider and no longer visible to the consumer of the value-added provider's service. The investment service mentioned above is an example of such a service. The second approach is where the wholesale service is offered directly to consumers by means of a *pass-through interface* , in which the primary functionality of the wholesaler's interface is presented directly to the consumer, but with the look and feel of the retailer's service. An example is a service that offers driving instructions between pairs of addresses. Many businesses with physical addresses may want to provide this service to their customers. However, such a service requires a means for setting the addresses and presenting the directions to the end consumer. These are fairly static input and output requirements, so the provider of the service may create a simple interface for these specific functions. With an appropriately designed interface structure, the retail provider could adapt this standard wholesale interface by overlaying it with certain service-specific presentation properties, like the retail service name, logo, presentation colors, and fonts. The result is an interface that presents the wholesaler's functionality, but looks and feels like part of the retailer's service.

8.3 Observations

There are a number of important lessons to be learned from the existing world of commercial activity. The following observations elucidate key elements for the successful facilitation of the information marketplace.
Observation 1. Market studies indicate that consumers are typically more interested in having their problems solved than in simply obtaining information. Furthermore, very few existing businesses focus on information retrieval. Instead, the large majority of businesses today exist to solve problems for their customers. Though there may be a substantial information retrieval task involved in the problem-solving, the service actually sold to the customer is almost always best characterized as a solution to the customers' problem(s).
The implications of this are important and drive providers, and consequently the supporting infrastructure, away from the retrieval of large quantities of information and toward the access of relevant problem-solving services. For example, the investment service mentioned above is more oriented toward problem-solving than the simple stock quote service upon which it relies. It may also focus much less on transporting raw information to its consumers and more on transporting

useful summaries or advice. Over the long term, this will be apparent in the increasing availability and popularity of "higher-level" problem-solving services, as discussed above. This shift will fundamentally change the ways information-based services work, and further motivate collaborative and cooperative services.

Also, these services will look more and more like problem-solvers over time, shifting the focus away from the appearance of "advertising" to one of "online presence". At the same time, there will be an increasing shift away from indexing *information* and toward indexing *services* on the network.

Observation 2. Markets are valued much more highly when they are perceived to be effectively ubiquitous in the array of services represented. For example, the perceived value of a yellow pages directory is directly related to the perceived ubiquity of the listings it contains - when customers believe that every potential provider is referenced. Thus, the information marketplace must be positioned to achieve and sustain near-ubiquity within some common regional boundaries, where the region may be defined by geography or domain. There are a number of important implications:

Observation 2a. The existing marketplace in a large metropolitan center has on the order of 100,000 businesses per 1,000,000 mass market consumers. Thus, the problem of scaling up to achieve ubiquity will be severe, and should occur relatively rapidly within the boundaries of the region. A network of this scale raises a number of additional issues, such as how consumers find appropriate services and quickly learn to use them. Proposed facilitation infrastructures must account for this.

Observation 2b. Approximately 85% of existing businesses are categorized as *small* businesses, and approximately 85% of these are owned and operated by a single individual. A large number of these smaller businesses and organizations are focused on providing local services to local consumers. Examples include plumbers, dry cleaners, churches, dentists, gas stations, bakeries, etc. These are not the types of businesses commonly viewed as "information services" companies, and many are not of general interest for distribution beyond their local region. However, they typically comprise the "heart" of local business communities, providing the types of everyday services that people are willing to pay for. Thus, we must carefully consider the needs of these types of potential providers. Specifically, there are large numbers of such businesses and organizations, and they typically exhibit different needs than the traditional "information services" organization.

Thus, while it is unlikely that small businesses, especially owner/operators, will be early adopters of emerging information commerce technologies, it is clear that they are essential for the achievement of ubiquity, and the ultimate success of the information marketplace. Thus, facilitators must carefully consider and account for their needs.

Observation 3. The ultimate potential of the technology cannot be achieved until access by mass market consumers is nearly ubiquitous. Businesses, especially the smaller, local businesses will be most likely to offer an online presence when there is broad availability to their customers. Yet mass market consumers will almost certainly want and need to use various different end-user devices to access services. In addition, there will almost certainly be various competing network architectures providing transport and related facilitation services. Thus, facilitation will require a service facilitation layer that "floats" on top of various network transport channels and capabilities, and services must be presentable on a variety of user devices with potentially divergent capabilities.

Observation 4. The modern shopping mall, much like the middle eastern souk, provides a distinct set of useful services to facilitate the interactions of commercial activity. It collects an attractive array of useful products and services into a single location. It provides a measure of personal comfort for its businesses' customers. It distributes the costs of these comforts (e.g., heating, air conditioning, and restrooms) and other amenities (e.g., advertising and special programs to attract customers). It offers a measure of safety. It provides a unified environment, including a certain look and feel, mode of behavior, and operating hours. Yet it allows each individual store to offer its own products and services in its own way. Each has the opportunity to provide its own unique aesthetic environment within the larger, coherent whole. Each is allowed to do business its own way, accepting the forms of payment it deems most suitable, offering its own sales and incentives to customers, hiring its own employees, and creating its own internal look and feel (e.g., friendliness, efficiency, personal touches). Basically, the mall provides an overall environment, which has its own characteristics designed to attract customers, yet stays out of the way when it comes to the ways the individual stores interact with their customers.

It seems likely that the same kinds of relationships will be valued in the information marketplace. The facilitators of the information marketplace must do the same kinds of things - facilitators must "make it possible" by creating an environment that attracts customers and supports a wide variety of business interactions without "getting in the way" or being seen as controlling those interactions. Facilitators must avoid getting into the business of telling businesses how to do business. Instead, they must make business interactions easy and safe in a relatively transparent way. They must provide the means and mechanisms for businesses to interact with their customers without controlling those interactions (i.e., the how, when, what, why, etc.).

In this view, the service functions provided by existing businesses to mass market consumers do not radically change. Instead, the changes occur primarily in the ways in which we interact with the providers of those services - using an electronic, information-based approach to solve many of the problems consumers encounter using today's systems, such as inconvenient time synchrony (e.g., the customer can only talk to the plumber when both are available), and the ability to rapidly distribute corrections and modifications in services (e.g., the business doesn't have to wait until the next edition of the yellow pages book).

8.4 Vision

As it evolves, the information marketplace will offer a number of attractive opportunities while allowing free market forces to shape future generations of information-based products and services. With an appropriate technological infrastructure as its foundation, the marketplace will favor the entrepreneurial providers and facilitators offering the best (e.g., highest value) approaches, as defined by consumers. Sheth and Sisodia provide a detailed examination of the sociological and economic aspects of the information marketplace [15].

The first wave of services in the information marketplace will be online versions of current businesses and services. It will be necessary for online services to compete, at least initially, with current practices. In competition, the online service must provide some competitive advantage, such as increased convenience, greater flexibility, greater visual impact, lower cost, reduced turnaround times, or increased utility. The online medium also offers opportunities to extend the types and levels of service that may be provided.

The observations lead us to expect the following trends over time in the information marketplace:

Toward greater online presence , and away from online advertising. The difference is primarily related to degree of interactivity. Online presence would involve some form of interaction with the intent of negotiating for or transacting commercial activity. In its early forms, we expect a number of legacy systems being transformed into online services, both to exploit the growing market and to leverage the large investments in such systems.

Toward new "facilitator" services that help consumers with their problem-solving activities. Such services might provide service registration and indexing to assist users in finding appropriate services (e.g., plumbers or appliance repair); ratings and referrals, presumably to enhance credibility of certain online services - a form of differentiation; comparative shopping to assist users in comparing the potential results of interacting with alternative providers; and online tracking, billing and payment services.

Toward new classes of problem-solvers that provide substantial added value to consumers. Examples include the following:

- Information wrappers, that hide information complexity and/or package information in more marketable or user-friendly forms. Such problem-solvers will be especially useful for repackaging legacy systems that provide substantial value, but are very difficult to use in current forms.

- Information brokers and clearinghouses that assist in collecting, categorizing, collating, clarifying, and correcting information and other types of services.

- Information filters, that apply salient properties of the user, the session, and/or the information to make reasonable, mostly automated decisions about which information or service is relevant. These pre-process information using historical references (past experience in the task), predictive heuristics (educated "guesses" about future performance), user responses (when in doubt, ask), knowledge of the information domain (will this information be helpful?), or some combination of these to prevent information overload in a human user.

- Gateway agents, to act as gateways to different types of service networks (i.e., based on different paradigms or approaches, or functioning on different network platforms.

- Decision-making aids that post-process information for specific tasks. Such tools digest, transform, collate, and/or interpret the information into a more easily assimilated package.

- Presentation and visualization tools that assist in determining the best way to present information, using computer graphics, animations, auditory feedback, or other means.

- User assistants and advocates that help users in various ways. Mass market users will not understand the intricacies of interface tools, the internal formatting of information, or the means by which information is accessed and distributed, so user assistants and advocates can perform complex tasks and represent the user's interests within the service network. Also, such agents might one day learn domain-specific knowledge of various services or service types, and use this to aid the consumer's access to these services.

Toward "local" communities , and away from all-encompassing global perspectives. Such communities may be based on area of interest or special needs, but it is likely that many such communities will be based on geography, with local services catering to local consumers.

8.5 Challenges

The collection of provider, consumer, and facilitation systems that support the information marketplace provide one example of *composite systems*, which exhibit the following characteristics: (1) they are comprised of a possibly very large number of individual entities, each of which is capable of performing one or more specific tasks as a standalone system; (2) these entities work together, and thus must be able to coordinate their actions and work cooperatively to solve problems that none can solve independently; and (3) their fundamental means of exchange is electronic - some form of information. As a result, entities must interoperate to the degree that they effectively communicate to share information, constraints, and goals. Such systems are typically distributed, geographically and/or organizationally, and are functionally heterogeneous, using different hardware and software for different tasks. Furthermore, these entities should perform cooperative tasks with minimal human intervention.

8.5.1 Technical Issues

The characteristics of composite systems impose a number of important constraints on the computing and communication infrastructure. In addition, systems that must be commercially viable add other requirements. These can be organized into the following types of challenges:

1. Composite systems require some form of interoperability and must account for the effects of *distribution* and *heterogeneity* among and between the entities. Such issues are typically addressed in the distributed and federated databases literature, and include type specification and conversion, distributed transactions and concurrency control, distributed access and coordination, data and knowledge semantics, and application-level semantics, constraints, and "correctness".

2. Composite systems exhibit the characteristics of open systems, as defined by Hewitt [5, 6], and must effectively operate in an environment of *concurrency* and *decentralization* . Such issues are typically addressed in the distributed artificial intelligence and cooperative systems literature, and include asynchronous communication, decentralized control, inconsistent information among entities, and inadequacy of the closed-world assumption.

3. Practical support systems are necessary for real-world deployment, and are necessary to provide *operations* and *support* functions in an operational environment. For example, the provider will want to protect and profit from his efforts, introducing the need for payment in exchange for services rendered. Issues include platform heterogeneity, user interfaces and presentation, authentication, security, privacy, transactions and orders, tracking and accounting, and payment and billing [7].

4. Also, the business environment is inherently characterized by frequent and rapid change. Thus, businesses require autonomy and functional independence, in an environment that is both *flexible* and *dynamic* . Flexibility allows them the freedom to do what they want in the way they want to do it. Dynamicity allows them to change it whenever they want. For example, it is often the case in business that innovation in marketing and sales is more important to success than innovation in products and services. Issues include functional autonomy and independence, functional flexibility to support broadly different and possibly divergent capabilities, and functional dynamicity, for rapid changes in functionality

8.5.2 Business Needs

The above considerations lead to the following technological needs for providers. These are critical to the successful (i.e., profitable) deployment of information commerce. Though providers will have other needs, we have chosen the following eight to focus on here.

1. *Individual Connectivity.* Each individual provider and consumer must have the basic capability to communicate with every other provider and consumer. In order to do this, each individual must have an inter-entity communication protocol and at least one common language by which meaningful semantic exchanges can occur. Shared language necessitates a shared vocabulary, or a set of terms within which this semantic exchange may be stated. This requires a minimal set of shared semantics. However, there are practical limits on the amount and types of semantics that can be shared a priori, at the creation of the entity, and clearly this must be relatively small. Thus, most application- or domain-specific semantics cannot be expressed in this language, and will require other languages. We thus turn to the notion of multiple, small languages that are designed around specific, generally narrow bands of functionality. In effect, they are designed to express concepts and terms for specific applications or domains (e.g., making reservations, leaving messages, negotiating prices and services, requesting data, etc.). Such languages need only be shared among those individual entities that must converse regarding that functionality. Since each entity must share the minimal language, and each may know any number of other domain languages, individual entities will generally be multilingual.

2. *Individual Identification/Location.* Individual entities require direct and unique addressability, which enables direct communication, and makes possible various kinds of support and facilitation services.

3. *Individual Independence.* Each individual entity must retain a reasonable degree of locality, such that each may have its own information, knowledge, and beliefs, which may be implicit. Knowledge about the internal design, naming, and workings of an individual entity remain internal, and should typically be independent of the communication languages. This allows the provider the freedom to change or replace the backend operations of the service with no change to the rest of the network - without notifications, upgrades to customer sites, or expensive software distribution. This introduces the need for translations between the communication language(s) and the languages the entity uses internally to process requests. Such translations are increasingly common and often yield favorable results when compared to the costs of incremental modifications that must be delivered widely to various "consumer" processes.
This form of locality allows the provider to modify his service with minimal disturbance to existing operations and practices, and with minimal change requirements in other entities that may interact with this one (e.g., as a wholesale buyer). It also allows the provider to use the right solutions and

tools for the right jobs. Because this locality includes the selection and use of hardware resources, it offers the freedom to use those devices that are most suitable for any given service. This policy in the network will result in rampant heterogeneity (i.e., below the level of the communication protocols and languages described above).

4. *Individual Autonomy.* In addition to the need for control over the internal organization of the entity, the provider must retain control over the operations of the entity. Each entity must be operationally autonomous, with its own processes and its own set of goals and priorities (possibly implicit). No outside entity can impose or supersede these without specifically contracting to do so. Thus, no facilitator or other entity, which may belong to someone else, can gain control of the provider's service, and control of the service stays in the hands of the provider.

5. *Individual Persistence.* Individual entities must exist through time so that they remain accessible and become known over extended periods of time. Ongoing availability is essential for many businesses. Also, a large number of businesses, especially those smaller ones that focus on personal service, will want to use individualized service histories to guide the current session with a given consumer. Thus, they must be capable of retaining a history of past contexts (i.e., sessions with a particular customer) for use in future contexts, and recalling those contexts when and as needed. Context retention may require the creation and ongoing revision of the context as multiple communication acts occur in a session.

6. *Individual Differentiation.* Within the limits of some global look and feel decisions, businesses must retain the ability to be different from their competitors. "One size fits all" won't work. This differentiation must occur in two areas:

   - *Content.* Individual entities must retain the ability to distribute their functions or content to the user. In other words, the provider must be able to differentiate his service on the basis of the properties of the service itself. This can take many forms, including the content of the text, images, and other media objects to be presented to consumers.
   - *Presentation.* Individual entities must also differentiate in terms of style and personality in their presentation, in much the same way that businesses differentiate themselves in various advertising media. Providers must be able to present their own sense of style, including personality-bearing information like colors and color schemes, display fonts and sizes, screen layouts, backgrounds, etc. The presentation must play on the user's device in a predictable fashion, without unnecessarily limiting the look, feel, or operation of the service.

7. *Individual Assurances.* Individual entities must receive reasonable assurances from the facilitation layer regarding performance during the rendering of service and appropriate payment for service.

   - *Tracking and Accounting.* Individual entities must be assured that their agreements with other entities will be properly tracked, accounted for, and paid for in a timely manner. Appropriate operations support systems must be built into the facilitation layer to log, backup, and manage communication acts, transactions, and other activities.
   - *Timeliness.* To be effective, the interactions between providers and consumers must exhibit certain predictable properties of response and throughput, and must account for the tracking and accounting mechanisms mentioned above.

8. *Individual Security.* Individual entities must have a reasonable level of security from attacks, either intentional or inadvertent. The following types of inter-related security services will be required:

   - *Privacy.* Since private information is generally given away only in order to receive some special consideration or advantage, it will be necessary for individual entities, especially those associated with end consumers, to protect such information to the greatest extent possible. Protocols for negotiating to receive such information will eventually be needed.
   - *Access Protection.* Providers with information that offers commercial advantage will not want to release that information or service without proper assurances that it will be duly paid for. One mechanism for achieving this is encryption, either during periods of latent storage or during network transmission.
   - *Intrusion Protection.* Both providers and consumers need assurances that the careless or malicious actions of others will not result in unwanted intrusions into their device(s). For example, there must be reasonable safety from the implantation of viruses or other destructive or uninvited programs.
   - *Authentication.* Some providers must be certain that they are talking to a known and authorized consumer. Thus, an authentication service will be necessary.
   - *Availability.* Eventually it will be necessary to implement support systems in the infrastructure to detect and prevent service jamming,

in which outside sources (possibly with malicious intent) seek to keep a service busy or otherwise limit its availability to its consumers, or to keep the service from reaching its consumers. Mechanisms that detect and/or prevent such actions will eventually become indispensable.

8.5.3 Future Needs

The following needs are similarly useful to those above, but are more difficult to define, due to two factors. First, there are many ways that these issues can be driven in the future, depending on how the information marketplace develops and what emerging technologies become viable in coming years. More experience and marketplace maturity is needed in order to understand market requirements, and greater technical maturity is necessary in order to know exactly what the technology can reasonably offer. Second, the relatively immature state of the technology causes a lack of general-purpose mechanisms for these tasks. Existing mechanisms tend to be constrained to specific applications or domains and therefore useful only under specific conditions. The range of conditions tends to be narrow, and not typically "naturally occurring", so it is difficult to apply them to real-life circumstances and situations. Thus the following appear to be quite useful, but for which we must wait, pending greater experience in the information marketplace and further technological progress.

Conversations, Contexts, and Histories. Because commercial activity is largely composed of ongoing conversations, involving context and history of past experiences, it is essential that the information marketplace support such capabilities. Thus, many individual entities will require mechanisms to support multi-message activities, to collect individual communication acts into ***conversations*** in a specific ***context***, and to collect these contexts into ***histories*** for subsequent use. Consequently, a mechanism is needed for associating individual messages with sessions, which can subsequently be linked to a historical context, if any. In addition, support for conversations and contexts should be key elements of service provider software. Long-term, history contexts, on the other hand, may be more application-dependent, and require mechanisms for specifying the types of information to be retained in the history and the ways in which historical contexts may be associated with current ones. This is a possible application for case-based reasoning. In any event, this function is *internal* to the service software.

Recovery Mechanisms. These would allow individual entities to recover from various kinds of interruptions due to unexpected failures in the network, in component hardware, or to the intermittent nature of mobile computing environments. These may be based on or related to the conversation and context mechanisms discussed above.

Negotiation and Contracting. Appropriate protocols and skills for various forms of negotiation and contracting would enable entities to dynamically arrange the conditions under which they work together. Again, this may require some form of the conversation and context mechanisms discussed above.

Cooperative Problem Solving. At some time in the future, some entities may need additional skills in complex, distributed problem solving activities related to coordinated, cooperative, or collaborative efforts. This will require mechanisms for negotiation and contracting.

Service Discovery. It will at some point be desirable for services to (semi-) automatically detect, probe, and "understand" other online services (e.g., newly available services).

Learning. Individual entities that are capable of automatically performing self-improvements over time offer certain advantages over the life-span of the individual entities. Such "learning" might involve better predicting future performance based on past experiences in similar situations or in working with certain other entities, or the inclusion of new features by having the entity self-discover available enhancements and auto-updating its capabilities.

8.5.4 Current Practices & Solutions

There is currently a surge of interest in information-based commerce, fueled largely by the convergence of the various technologies supporting the World Wide Web (WWW), including the Hypertext Markup Language (HTML), the Hypertext Transfer Protocol (HTTP), and a growing variety of hypertext client and server engines. The following is a brief assessment of these with respect to the eight needs identified above.

The web presents some limitations in its current form. Among these is the inability to provide bandwidth and/or throughput guarantees. Thus, it cannot currently assure levels of performance to either providers or consumers, inhibiting the performance assurance needs of suppliers in information commerce. In addition, three other, existing networks may play roles in the future: the public switched telephone network; the broadcast network, including television, cable, and satellite systems; and utility networks, including the electrical power distribution grid and their control networks. The industries surrounding each of these are exploring various ways of providing facilitation services, and each has expressed some degree of interest in information commerce as an appropriate application domain for their network. the future impact of these is unknown.

The appeal of the web is due primarily to the flexible design, radical simplicity, and low-cost availability of the protocols and various HTML display engines, or browsers, which are designed for extreme ease-of-use for both providers and consumers. Since HTML is based on a hypertext document paradigm, use of the system involves requesting, downloading, and displaying HTML documents on the user's screen by a browsing/display engine. It was recently extended to display forms and accept forms-like input. Only three types of information are allowed in HTML: information to be presented directly to the user (i.e., the document itself), interface navigation options and commands (i.e., to manipulate the interface itself), and upstream commands, including document retrieval commands and forms input, which are transported over the network to a remote server. This design is both safe from the perspective of the client machine and elegant in its simplicity.

However, the web's current limitations become more apparent in applications that are fundamentally *outside* the world of documents, yet are *inside* the world of electronic commerce. Among these are the following:

- HTTP lacks a notion of "session" - it is strictly single message oriented, rather than conversation or context oriented. Although it is possible to build a session mechanism using the standard widgets, HTTP itself does not currently provide this. This may be resolved in future versions.

- HTML's document metaphor is based on very loosely coupled relationships between client and server, or between browser and document, and as a result lacks an adequate notion of interactivity for many applications associated with information-based commerce [2]. Because it is based on the notion of fetching and retrieving documents, interactive operations such as editing or annotating sections of the presentation are not possible.

- The web uses a fundamental "pull" model of retrieval, as opposed to a "push" model. Information is only obtained when it is explicitly asked for, rather than when it is relevant or needed. There is no mechanism for "subscribing" to information or services and receiving them as they become available. Current email systems, based on a simple push model, lack the utility of the web.

- HTML is based on the fundamental notion of client control over the document's presentation, so most presentation variables are under the direct control of the client. While this may be acceptable for documents, for which the fonts or the color of the "paper" and "ink" are generally less than critical, it is less attractive for business services that seek to be differentiated from their competitors. Expressive aesthetics are critical to this differentiation, yet providers receive no assurances about how the presentations will appear on the user's device. Instead, this is a function of the capabilities of the user's device, the capabilities of the transport channel, and the way the user has set up the interface variables to control fonts, sizes, colors, and whether and how various types of media objects are presented.

- HTML effectively limits the types of interface widgets that can be used in a presentation to those included in the version currently in common use. The needs for business differentiation, especially in an evolving marketplace, will be better served by a capability for dynamically extending

[2] The extension of HTML to include a forms capability allows providers to receive input from the user, which is a limited form of interactivity. However, the "upstream" message containing information entered into the forms is transmitted in a batch mode (i.e., all at once, rather than a character, word, or field at a time). Much more dynamic styles of interactivity are required for unrestricted information commerce.

the set of interface widgets through the use of a widget specification language. Clearly, this capability will increase the size and complexity of the presentation engine. However, its absence reduces the provider's ability to innovate in the design and delivery of service presentations.

Thus, while the web tools were very well designed, they were designed for uses other than those that will ultimately be required in the information marketplace. A large and growing segment of the mass market consumer population is already familiar with a different metaphor that better addresses the needs of business providers - that of interactive computing. Current approaches must either be substantially extended or replaced altogether in order to support these kinds of activities. The following section presents one approach to this.

8.6 Approach

Based on the observations above, our intent is to move away from the basic notion of information retrieval toward the notion of interactive computing. In doing so, our philosophy is to address the needs stated in section 3 with a "best current practices" approach, using the best known solutions to get started, building these in such a way that they can be enhanced, extended, or replaced in the future as new ideas emerge, then making those improvements when the time is right. In addition, we will take an approach similar to that taken in the WWW: a flexible design, the greatest possible simplicity, and near-ubiquitous distribution.
There are four main elements in our approach:

1. The first is to create a "facilitation layer" based on the notion of *multiple cooperating agents* [3]. This layer is comprised of a software infrastructure that supports both providers and consumers, and upon which providers can build services. These agents have the basic properties described above, being autonomous, independent, persistent, etc. The information marketplace can thus be viewed and implemented as a community of cooperating agents.

2. The second component is a *functional access language* (FAL), or group of languages, to provide consumers with mechanized (i.e., machine-oriented) access to the provider, presumably to request, solicit, or invoke the provider's service. This is a mechanized access language for getting the provider's agent to perform its service.

3. The third is an *interface description language* (IDL) that provides consumers with manual (i.e., human-oriented) access to the provider. This allows the provider to specify a user interface through which consumers can interact with the provider's service in ways that are defined and for the most part controlled by the provider.

[3] The notion of agents has become ambiguous during the past few years. Our definition is given below.

4. The fourth is a series of *special facilitation agents*, that offer special services in support of the other agents' operations and transactions. Δ

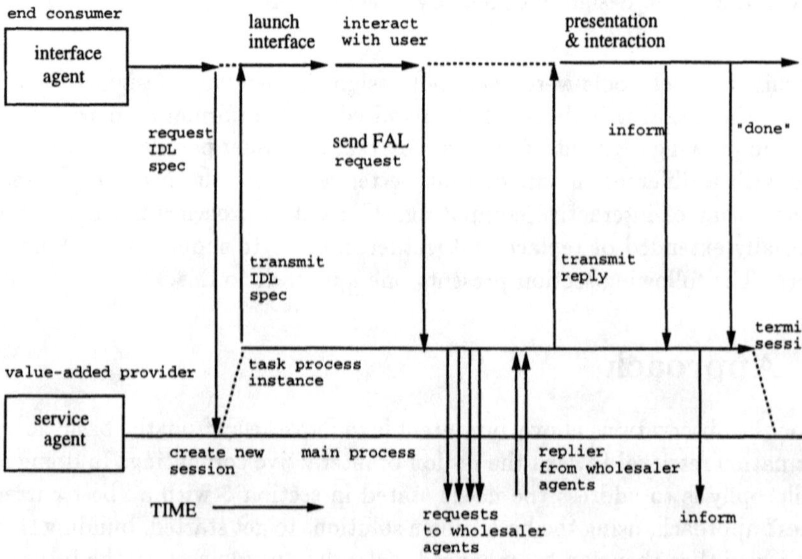

Figure 8.4: Figure 4. Interactions between the interface agent and the service agent.

Collectively, these components can be made to resolve many of the target business needs. The agents, in providing and consuming services, send messages using the FALs. Figure 4 shows an example of a typical series of interactions. Human consumers see and interact with individual services in ways that are defined by the provider using the IDL. In a typical scenario with a human consumer, the human begins a session with a specific provider by requesting that provider's interface. This is downloaded from the provider to the consumer's device and launched. The user interacts with the interface in various ways to accomplish her task. This may include navigating through the interface itself, or it may involve sending messages to the provider's service and possibly receiving responses. Such network activities would typically be completely transparent to the human user, being defined by the user's actions (e.g., text typed to the interface, buttons pushed, etc.), then formatted into the appropriate FAL and transmitted by the user's interface agent. After receiving these messages, the service agent handles them, possibly by invoking various wholesale services provided by others, and returns replies if required. Any number of side effects may occur as needed, including messages to archiving and transaction tracking agents and other operations support functions. Replies received from the provider's service are handled by the interface agent, and may be presented to the user as appropriate, though this is not necessary. This is conceptually very similar to the approach currently taken in the WWW, but allows for a broader range of

interaction types, and better supports the notion of interactive sessions.
For some services, it may not be necessary or appropriate for human users to interact directly, so the provider need not specify a human interface using the IDL.

8.6.1 Interacting Agents

In this approach, each agent is an autonomous individual within a large society of other individuals. Each individual is capable of interacting with others in some way to solve problems. Each adheres to societal "norms" of behavior. Each possesses its owns skills and abilities, which it makes available to the society. The agents provide a layer of ***virtual homogeneity*** within which advanced concepts like negotiation and cooperation can be built, and above which a new and broad range of functional heterogeneity can be constructed. This approach is very similar to that known as ***agent-based software engineering*** [4].
This layer supports interactive computing, yet is very flexible, allows extensions, and does not significantly limit the range of applications that may be deployed. Insofar as possible, this layer should be built on the same notions of radical simplicity, ease of use, and ready distribution that the WWW offers.

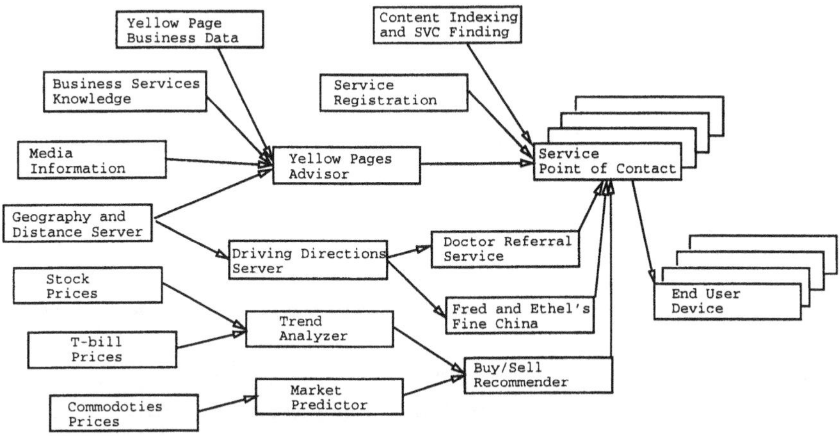

Figure 8.5: Figure 5. A peer-to-peer architecture for the information marketplace, showing wholesale and retail services and value-added relationships among the services., which are made available to mass market consumers.

In a typical information marketplace, we expect to see an arrangement of the form shown in Figure 5, where a large number of providers are available to a large number of consumers for a variety of wholesale, retail, and related interactions. These agents are both conceptually and practically autonomous, and thus interact on a peer-to-peer basis. In this view, agents are conceptually stationary, interacting by exchanging messages rather than by traveling around the network

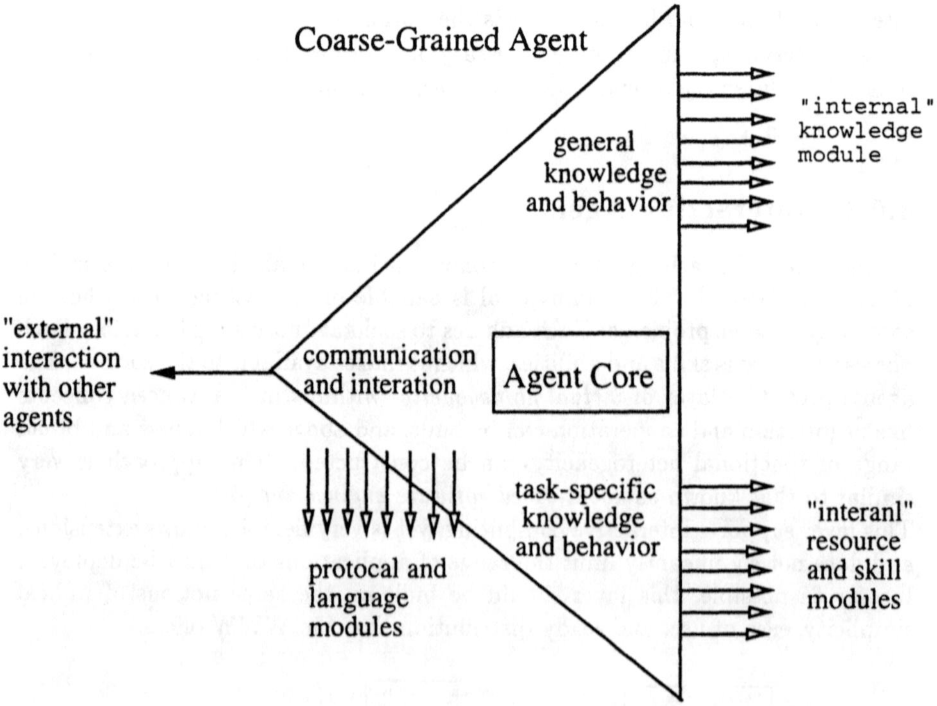

Figure 8.6: Figure 6. The functional components of an agent, as seen in the Coarse-Grained Agent system.

The Coarse-Grained Agent (CGA) system, originally developed to support cooperative information systems, has been adapted [7, 8, 10, 11, 12] in order to support laboratory exploration of interactions and services for information commerce.

CGAs are based on a simple conceptual model for extensible agents, as shown in Figure 6. Each CGA has three main components: *communication* - the ability to interact with other agents using shared protocols and languages; *local , task-specific knowledge and behavior* - the ability to perform one or more task-specific activities (this can be viewed as a set of *skills*); and *general knowledge and behavior* - the ability to perform general task-independent "social" behaviors such as negotiation, cooperative planning, prioritizing tasks, reason-

[4]The notion of functionally stationary agents does not preclude an ability to move from one machine to another, as long as that movement is not essential to the agent's fundamental operation, as is the case with some agent systems that require agents to move about a network as an essential part of performing their tasks. Instead, this approach allows for a form of ambulation that is intended more for load balancing purposes than as a metaphor for distributed problem solving.

ing about agent-internal capabilities, predicting future performance, recovering from unexpected difficulties, modeling external agents and functionalities, and the like. This component captures the behaviors most closely resembling *intellect.* [5] Individual agents may vary widely in these capabilities. For example, simple server-like agents may require no general knowledge capabilities (with the possible exception of certain simple capabilities that may one day be part of the minimal definition of an agent). The three components of a CGA are linked together by the *agent core*, which acts as "glue" to hold the three components and their modules together, providing support for general operations such as asynchronous message sending and receiving, multitasking, and shared memory between tasks.

The definition of CGAs is based on a minimal set of societal norms, or necessary and sufficient behaviors, which are implemented in one or more of these components. This definition will change over time, as the needs of the marketplace become better understood and as new technologies become available. Each of these components is designed to be extended as new technologies and tools emerge. As a result, each of the three components of an agent may be viewed as a series of empty "plugs" into which tools may be placed to extend the functionality of the agent.

Communication and Interaction Modules

CGA communication currently depends on the existence of a byte-stream communication service. All higher level communication functions make use of this underlying facility. Any lower level protocol capable of providing byte-stream service can be used to implement the network communication required. In the future this requirement may be relaxed to allow CGA communication using protocols based on different communication metaphors.

Above the byte-stream service there is a simple message transport protocol for routing and delivering messages directly from one agent to another. This protocol uses a *postal metaphor*, and is used by a collection of mail handlers that run on participating host machines.

The agent coordination protocol (ACP), providing information regarding the message itself, is implemented above the message transport protocol. ACP provides information about the message directly to the recipient agent. It is an extension of the Contract Net protocol [16], and provides information regarding the session to which the message is associated, the names of the recipient agents, and timing and other constraints regarding processing and replies.

The message itself is transported in a single field within the ACP, and contains the semantic intent, expressed in some FAL, through which the sending and receiving agents interact with each other. A detailed examination of the CGA communication system, including the metaphors and protocols used in the CGA system, and a simple example FAL are described in [10].

[5] Note that humans fit within this conceptual view - an important consideration as we move toward an environment in which machines and humans work together cooperatively to accomplish information commerce.

Task-Specific Knowledge and Behavior

Each of the agents in the network has a reason to exist, which is essentially to encapsulate and make available some particular function or set of functions. These functions are internal to the agent, and are accessed using a FAL. The agent thus becomes a contractor with respect to that functionality, offering a particular *skill* or *resource* that may not be available elsewhere. Thus, agents are viewed as *skill-based* entities. The agent's skills consist of one or more functionalities, ranging from the very simple (e.g., controlling a simple robot arm, or a matrix multiplier on a high-speed parallel computer), to the very complex (e.g., finding and assembling complex information from numerous sources, analyzing it, and recommending actions). Because this is implemented via a series of plug-in modules, it is possible for nearly any function to be present. With appropriate tools for creating agents and embedding these functions within them, online services may be constructed very quickly.

For provider agents, the encapsulated skill(s) will involve the provision of some service or set of services, possibly based on special purpose hardware or software resources. Provider agents can be made to "wrap" legacy information systems, retrofitting them for the information marketplace and allowing providers to further leverage their historical investments in these systems.

For end consumer agents, the skill will be representing the user's interests in various ways, including finding and accessing appropriate services, downloading those services' interfaces, and possibly negotiating on behalf of the user.

General Knowledge and Behavior

The types of capability modules in this component are by far the least mature and the least understood. Consequently, this is the area in which the greatest change is expected in the future. Some of the more intriguing areas in which useful progress may be made are those described in section 5.3: contexts and histories, recovery mechanisms, negotiation and contracting, cooperative problem solving, service discovery, and learning. Other areas include general data and knowledge stores, reasoning, and knowledge of social behaviors.

Most of what can be included here would be considered overhead processing, and should arguably not be included in the minimal capabilities of CGAs. Research on these issues is not yet conclusive, so it is not clear which components are necessary and which should be optional.

Agent "Core"

The CGA *agent core* provides a set of agent abstractions by which developers of provider, consumer, and facilitator agents can construct new agents easily, and without the need to look below the level of the agent abstractions. This includes functions for sending, receiving, and queuing messages, awaiting replies, spawning new tasks, attaching replies to existing tasks, recovering from task failures, external monitoring of internal activities for troubleshooting, and defining new FALs, including a simple FAL parser. There are high-level functions for wrapping behavioral code with this agent functionality, and for creating and killing agents. The core has functions for performing a variety of useful operations on tasks, which are represented as processes on the host computer. It also includes place holder functions for agent cloning and ambulation to support effectiveness and load balancing. For a more detailed discussion of the CGA architecture, see [8].

8.6.2 Functional Access Languages

Functional access languages (FALs) are designed around the expression of a particular set of functionalities. They provide the means by which a consumer, or more typically an agent working on the consumer's behalf, interact with the service agent(s) to access and use the service. These may be generalized languages that express functionality around a *type of application*, like CycL for knowledge representation [13], or they may be specialized languages that express domain-dependent functionality around a *specific domain*, like accessing a legacy database containing historical product revenue information [11]. Basically, FALs can be designed for any purpose a provider desires. Neither the syntax nor the semantics are limited to any globally-defined form. This offers a number of advantages to the provider in defining, marketing, and selling a particular service, especially when it involves the use of legacy information, resources, or skills.

This poses an obvious and difficult problem to consumers and their agents - what are the syntax and semantics of these languages, and how can these be discovered without specific a priori knowledge of the language? There are two ways to do this: (1) *manual discovery*, a priori, via some form of publication (online or hardcopy), which is subsequently typed directly by a user (a possibly difficult task, since the syntax and vocabulary may not be human-friendly) or hardcoded into some form of access program. This approach is static, and fails to address several of the needs of the information marketplace. (2) *automated discovery*, where agents share languages and mechanisms that enable one agent to express to another the syntax and semantics of a "new" language (i.e., the one being "learned"), such that the learning agent is subsequently able to correctly express requests for services using that language. No solution to this problem is currently known.

However, there is a practicable alternative: manual discovery done by the provider of the service, then embedded within a distinct user interface, such that certain specific manipulations of the interface produce syntactically and semantically correct messages to be sent to the provider's service in the FAL. This effectively hides the syntax and semantics of the FAL within the interface, and thereby minimizes the knowledge and semantics that must be shared, at least for end

consumer use of the service. This may be better characterized as a form of discovery avoidance, since the provider, who supplies the consumer interface, already knows the FAL.
In order to accomplish this we need the third element of our solution - a suitable IDL, which provides an interface between the user and the service, and in so doing hides the details of the FAL from consumers. Interfaces in the IDL are created and maintained by the provider as a typically essential part of service provision.

8.6.3 Interface Description Language

The interface description language (IDL) is designed to provide a mechanism by which a user may interact with a service in ways meaningful to humans. The IDL provides a machine-independent description of the provider's customer interface, such that when the consumer interacts with the provider's service, the provider is assured that some reasonably faithful rendition of his interface is presented to the user and is behaving in the manner intended by the provider.
To do this, the IDL must capture not only the content of the service, but also most of the details regarding look and feel, including specifications for the following types of information regarding service presentation:

- screen layout, with relative and/or absolute positions of widgets and content
- fonts, including styles, sizes (possibly relative), and definitions when necessary
- colors, color sets, and textures for text, highlighting, backgrounds, etc.
- custom icons and other media objects
- interface widgets, including the specification of new widgets
- interface navigation behaviors for various widgets, like scrollers, buttons, button groups, icons, tool panes, etc.
- functionality access behaviors to compose and transmit messages to the provider's service agent

The display engine that "runs" the IDL, which resides on the user's device, must limit the definition of interface behaviors, especially in specifications of functionality access and new widgets, to the following types of behavioral primitives: presentation of content (i.e., various text or media objects), execution of interface navigation commands (to manipulate the interface itself), and generation of FAL statements and requests (to be sent over the network to a remote agent for servicing). Though somewhat different in functionality, this approach is quite similar to that taken in the design of the WWW, and offers similar safety from the spread of viruses and other destructive and unwanted programs to user devices.

This capability adds a functional requirement for most provider and consumer agents - a language that allows a consumer agent to request and receive from the provider a suitable interface, written in the IDL. Also, auxiliary services, such as temporarily downloading fonts as required for a specific interface without forfeiting copyrights, are necessary.

8.6.4 Special Facilitation Agents

As discussed in section 5.2, there are a number of operations support and related needs for information-based commerce. Many of these may be usefully viewed and implemented as special agents whose internal skill in some way provides one or more facilitation tasks. These are known as *facilitation agents*, and are implemented using the same agent software and communications subsystems used by providers and consumers. For example, special agents could exist primarily to register services or provide content-based indexing and access, as shown in figure 5. Other possible facilitation agents might offer calculation of usage fees or taxes, network traffic monitoring, resource discovery, service and/or user registration and indexing, information and service filters, archiving and recovery services, billing support, security vouchers and/or timestamps, public key repositories, and digital cash and electronic payment services.

This approach allows further reuse of the agent mechanisms, and at the same time offers an attractive form of homogeneity and consistency in the overall environment. It also provides a homogeneous mechanism for deploying facilitation services that places all potential providers of such services on an equal footing. No longer will the suppliers of the underlying networks have distinct competitive advantages in these kinds of services. This will encourage open competition among facilitation venders, and eventually lead to better services at lower costs for both consumers and providers.

Also, facilitation agents can be upgraded and enhanced independently of the rest of the infrastructure, enabling easier transitions to new or improved capabilities in the facilitation layer, just as it enables easier transitions for other kinds of services.

8.7 Implementation

The application prototype, known as Raven, was developed to explore the issues of and technological solutions for information commerce on a broad scale, and especially oriented toward smaller businesses and mass market consumers. It includes the following classes of agents: *user agents*, for running the IDL engine; *point-of-contact agents*, for managing the heterogeneities of the provider's and the consumer's platforms; *facilitation agents*, for assisting consumer agents in locating and accessing provider agents, managing transactions, tracking and accounting, etc.; and ***service agents***, for representing providers' services to consumers.

Various of these agents run on various computer platforms concurrently, including Symbolics Lisp machines, Macintoshes, and Sun workstations. There are two fundamentally different implementations of CGAs to support this, written in Lisp and C, which use slightly different versions of the CGA model, but have identical minimal behaviors.

This application was built in a relatively short period of time by leveraging an existing CGA implementation, as developed for a different application. Developers of the service agents for individual businesses were never required to look below the level of the agent metaphor and implementation in designing this overall system, reaping a substantial savings in time and expense in the development of a relatively complex set of agents and interactions. More details about this application are given in [7, 9].

8.8 Discussion

8.8.1 General

The approach described above addresses many of the needs that have been identified for the information marketplace. The multi-agent software engineering strategy addresses the issues of concurrency and decentralization. The agent communication protocols and the underlying message transport services manage physical distribution transparently by providing each agent with a unique network "address" and corresponding connectivity with other agents. The agent architecture provides suitable mechanisms for independence, autonomy, and persistence, so providers can own and maintain an online presence.

Many of the thorny heterogeneity issues related to semantic interoperability are avoided through the use of multiple, small FALs, which are distributed by means of human-oriented interfaces specified in the IDL. The FALs also limit the size of vocabulary and amount of knowledge that must be shared between agents a priori. There are no currently known semantic models that span the enormous range of existing commercial services, much less the range that may exist in the future as new and unpredictably innovative services are created. Even if there were such a model, it would be too large to reasonably embed in all practical user systems and maintain over time. Thus, a scheme that minimizes the requirements for shared semantics is prudent and facilitates a more dynamic environment in which services are more easily added, removed, and changed.

In the future it may become desirable to include mechanisms for enhancing or extending the minimal shared knowledge of CGAs automatically, either with or without human intervention. However, this is a problematic operation, as shared knowledge tends to diverge over time, leading to the potentially serious problems related to incorrectly assumed levels of shared knowledge.

The IDL is designed to offer providers the opportunity to differentiate themselves on the basis of presentation look and feel as well as content. As a result, businesses have the opportunity to present their service in their own way. The IDL should eventually support a variety of heterogeneous hardware environments, from hand-held "personal digital assistants" to high-capability computing platforms, to continuous media streaming devices such as set-top boxes.

This approach allows an immense range of flexibility, in both functionality and presentation, and creates a very dynamic environment in which services can come and go frequently. It is essential, in order to reach ubiquity among providers of services, that the environment support the breadth of types of services currently available in the commercial world. Furthermore, it is essential for future innovation in sales, marketing, and presentation, that the information marketplace accommodate types of services and presentations that cannot yet be predicted.

This approach provides another benefit - the IDL effectively "hides" the consumer's device and software from the provider, and the FAL "hides" the provider's device and software from the consumer. This architectural disconnect allows for a wide variety of heterogeneous devices and software to coexist, coordinate, and work cooperatively across a large network.

The approach discussed here is more flexible than that in the WWW, but also somewhat more difficult to use, for both providers and consumers. Because this approach provides greater functionality, it requires greater complexity in the consumer and provider engines. However, this approach does not necessarily replace the WWW - it is best viewed as yet another network tool, albeit a more dynamic and interactive one. Furthermore, it does not require a specific transport network, but can work on a variety of networks, including the Internet, the public switched telephone network, various digital narrowband networks, such as integrated services digital network (ISDN), and various broadband networks.

This architecture by itself does not directly address other key issues, however. This approach also does not address the timeliness of service deliveries for information and media objects. This issue is better addressed in the network itself, and is thus beyond the scope of this chapter. However, it may be necessary for the inclusion of mechanisms at the agent level to negotiate regarding these deliveries, then interact with the underlying network (or agents representing the underlying network) to obtain the necessary guarantees.

This architecture also does not provide security services. With the addition of one or more encryption schemes, interagent communication can be augmented to provide access protection and authentication. The design of the IDL and its runtime engine minimizes the opportunity for unwanted intrusions of viruses and other destructive programs that may be piggybacked on legitimate messages. Privacy is in many regards a social issue, best addressed by non-technical means such as legal restrictions on the uses of the kinds of information that will be available to both providers and consumers. However, user agents, which represent the interests of consumers, provide a place within which privacy protections may be implemented. These agents can conceivably be fitted with filters for giving out information only when it is relevant for some transaction, and thereby

reduce the size of the privacy problem by limiting the number of outside entities that have access to information. Similarly, provider agents can be implemented to prevent unauthorized accesses.
We will eventually need some mechanism for guaranteeing availability. Recently, two cases of service jamming have been observed in the Internet - a "hunter-killer" program that seeks and destroys certain targeted messages; and a procedure whereby legitimate mailboxes are "flooded" with junk mail to overrun the service and prevent timely handling of serious messages. Mechanisms to detect and/or prevent such occurrences will most probably be developed as specific needs arise. It is possible that some of these may be best implemented as facilitation agents.

8.8.2 Agents

The notion of agents as described herein is useful in two distinct ways. First, it provides an intuitive *metaphor* for devising distributed, heterogeneous problem-solving systems. The metaphor is the model by which developers and providers think about services and their consumers. Second, when implemented it provides a practicable *mechanism* that substantially reduces the cognitive load on developers of services. The mechanism is basically a set of tools that developers and providers employ to solve problems. The metaphor and mechanism combine to form a useful approach to software engineering for the information marketplace

Metaphor

The agent metaphor is that of a "society" comprised of large numbers of rather capable individuals, each specializing in one or more specific resources or skills. Potentially complex social interactions involving many individuals are often required in this setting. In this view the agent takes on anthropomorphic qualities, making the approach quite intuitive to humans.
The agent metaphor offers three useful properties. First, it provides an *intuitive abstraction* which closely resembles the socially-oriented world of human activities. As a result, human problem solvers can more easily conceptualize and implement solutions to difficult or distributed problems. Second, the agent metaphor provides a *coordination model*, useful for linking together providers and consumers. This model is both explicit and separable, allowing incremental development, deployment, maintenance, and enhancement as new or improved models emerge. While this model is not yet complete, it provides a reasonable place to begin to deploy distributed systems. Third, the agent metaphor offers *conceptual separability*. Not only is the model and its implementation separable from other technological elements of the overall system, but the individual entities are conceptually and effectively separable from each other, providing the benefits of separate updates and improvements, separate tools and techniques, separate capabilities, and separate ownership. These benefits, along with the resulting capacity for independence and autonomy in individual agents, offer

significant potential for business and commercial applications.
This metaphor provides a general framework within which services, especially traditional information retrieval services, can disappear into the problem-solving fabric (i.e., become transparent by virtue of either IDL interfaces or by wholesale selling to retail services), allowing human consumers to concentrate on relevant "higher" problems instead of distracting them with information retrieval tasks.
In traditional distributed problem-solving systems, a typically large portion of the implementation is dedicated to handling interactions and data conversions between and among entities. Maintaining this can be a costly, labor-intensive problem over the lifespan of the overall system. Agents encapsulate many of these operations into code which is separable from the individual services and interfaces in that it can be separately upgraded and maintained with little or no change to the basic services and interfaces. In this way, agents are a conceptual extension to the notion of object-oriented programming (OOP), and offer many of the same benefits to the information marketplace that OOP systems bring to programming [1, 14, 17].

Mechanism

The agent mechanism offers several practical advantages for the development and distributed deployment of services in the information marketplace. It drives the intellectual benefits of the agent metaphor into the development of specific applications by providing a layer of *virtual homogeneity*. This layer offers a known, homogeneous layer of shared capabilities, knowledge, and functionality through which large numbers of individual services can be quickly deployed. There may be broad heterogeneity below this layer, both in the communication networks used and in the computing platforms upon which the agents reside, and a broad functional heterogeneity above this layer, in the specific resources and skills represented by agents.
The agent mechanism is a fully reusable implementation of the virtual homogeneity described above. As such, it is domain independent, and can be widely distributed as the agent foundation for providers, consumers, and facilitators.
It enables easy distribution of solutions by "wrapping" one or more specific skills with the coordination and cooperation models discussed above. With the addition of a suitable FAL and IDL-based interface, a service can be available for distributed, asynchronous access by consumers with relatively little effort. With appropriate auxiliary facilitation services for registration and service finding, the service can be accessible online in a matter of seconds or minutes of being ready for access.
This "wrapping" behavior allows for the rapid distribution of services based on either new or legacy systems, and allows businesses to leverage their existing or legacy systems in a new format and possibly to a much larger group of consumers. This distribution can be as wide as the underlying network upon which it is based.
The modularity and separability of the architecture allow for easy distribution

of agent updates to various remote sites. With suitable additions to the minimal agent language, or through vendor-dependent languages, agents could be made to update themselves automatically as new versions of the agent software become available. This allows for easy distribution of agent mechanism upgrades and enhancements as new capabilities are developed.

This mechanism is based on a completely open architecture. Once the necessary and sufficient requirements for the entities are published, anyone can build and sell agent software that will interoperate in this environment. Furthermore, a large variety of organizations may define niche markets in this environment (e.g., special consumer agents, special agents for various classes of provider services, such as catalog shopping services or wholesale purchasing services).

Because the agent mechanism is effectively separable from the internal skills of the agent, and the internal design is effectively separable from the FAL, providers can upgrade or modify the back end of their services (e.g., to change host computing platforms) with little or no changes to the agent mechanism, the FAL, or the IDL interface [6] . This facilitates a very general "plug and play" environment.

The autonomy and independence of the agent mechanism allow service providers to retain physical autonomy, independence, and ownership of their own information and services.

8.8.3 Disadvantages

There are some properties of this approach that may be disadvantageous in some situations. First, there are a number of properties that may combine to slow service response times:

- the transport speed and throughput of the underlying network(s)
- the efficiency of the agent software on the provider's device, and the load on the device
- the efficiency and effectiveness of the provider agent's internal "skills"
- the level of indirection required in the wholesale/retail chain during runtime - services that cache information from their suppliers will typically run faster than those that must access the supplier for each retail request. Runtime indirection should generally be avoided whenever possible in the creation of wholesale services. Of course, this will not be possible when the information is dynamic, such as in the raw stock quote service mentioned earlier. In such cases it is imperative that the wholesale service and its network connection be as fast as possible to provide the shortest response times to retail consumers.

---

[6] This is only true to the extent that the interaction language for accessing the agent has not been modified. Language modifications are effectively changes in the interface, and require appropriate changes in all agents which use that language through means other than the IDL interfaces.

Second, true device independence is difficult in an environment where the devices have too great a range of capabilities. Possible user devices in the information marketplace can range from the old-fashioned rotary dial telephone to televisions with set-top boxes to wireless hand-held assistants to high-end computer systems. It may be necessary to define an ontology of capabilities and classify devices accordingly. Providers might then define different interfaces for different classes of consumer devices.
Third, this approach requires near-ubiquity in the marketplace in order to achieve its ultimate potential. This poses a "chicken-and-egg" problem. The means by which we effect the transition from current architectures to this new approach are unknown.
Fourth, in attempting to achieve ubiquity this approach imposes a specific environment on the providers, consumers, and facilitators of services. Though it may not be the only approach available, it cannot achieve its potential unless it is nearly ubiquitous. However, the paradigm captured by this approach is well-known and widely used in existing markets. In this regard, this approach may be an advantage.

8.8.4 Summary

The approach taken in this work, when deployed, will facilitate a free-market environment for the creation and distribution of information and problem-solving services. The result will be a continual evolution of profitable, consumer-oriented services, in which the winners are determined by free market forces.
This approach enables the creation of layered wholesale and retail services, which in turn promotes the development of higher-level, value-added problem-solving services. Over time, both providers and consumers should have access to services that are significantly more useful and less expensive than those available under other deployment scenarios. Furthermore, this approach creates new entrepreneurial opportunities for a variety of new kinds of layered facilitation and problem-solving services.
From the provider's perspective, this approach meets several critical needs, including the foundational notions of local ownership and control of services - facilitators can effectively operate without either dictating or controlling the services.
Experience with laboratory prototypes and customer marketing for several related applications indicates that what we propose is practically achievable and can be made to support real-world commercial interactions.

8.9 Future Work

However, this approach is not without its risks. Much work remains in order to address these:
Definition. The minimal definition of CGAs needs to be very carefully and deliberately revisited and redesigned with a clear orientation toward the information marketplace. Also, a suitable IDL must either be found or designed to support the requisite functions.
Development. The current CGA implementation is not ready for deployment. It was originally intended only for laboratory use, and requires substantial additional work. In development, it may be beneficial to thoroughly review the infrastructure design in order to consider replacing much of the CGA support protocols and mechanisms with similar tools in KQML [2, 3]. Certain basic support functions may be replaced with more generic Internet-based services as well, such as using mail protocols or an upgraded HTTP to replace the CGA message transport subsystem. Also, a suitable IDL engine for various consumer devices must be found or constructed. If possible, it would be useful for such an engine to also display HTML documents in a built-in document-style interface, for compatibility with HTML-based services. Suitable security mechanisms must also be adopted or developed.
Support Tools. If the environment we envision is to ever approach the goal of near-ubiquity in terms of existing businesses, it will be necessary to provide tools to support rapid service creation and easy maintenance, by organizations with little or no technical expertise. Approaches to this have been suggested but not yet implemented. Facilitation Agents. In order to fully support commercial activities, several facilitation agents and support subsystems must be developed.
Field Trials. In order to determine the effects of scaling up to real-world proportions, one or more community-sized field trials will be necessary. This will both stress the infrastructure design and provide realistic marketing information, which is necessary given that the results of traditional marketing techniques have been inconsistent in related applications.
Emerging Technologies. Though we have argued against including advanced techniques in the minimal definition of CGAs, it may nonetheless be desirable in the future to include some of these as optional "plug-ins" for inclusion as appropriate for specific agents and applications. Modules for agent negotiation, agent modeling, and performance predictions are likely candidates.

8.10 Conclusions

This chapter has presented a vision for an information marketplace and explored some of the technical challenges facing those who would realize it. Specifically we have looked at technical solutions for embedding services in the network and allowing them to coordinate their actions and interact with consumers. This approach offers enormous potential for information commerce by focusing on the needs of providers, especially those smaller businesses with few resources to spend and little expertise with respect to the foundational technologies. Laboratory prototypes and experiments to date have yielded positive results, indicating general feasibility, though with associated risks. Market tests indicate strong provider interest among smaller businesses. Thus, we conclude that this approach is reasonable, and should be further explored.

8.11 Acknowledgments

This work would not have been possible without innumerable discussions with colleagues over the past five years. Rick Blumenthal and Bill McIver were instrumental in the design and implementation of the CGA platforms, as well as in the applications. Mari Power, Bill Stack, Adam Marx, Judi Hand, and Irene Rosenthal provided ongoing support, insight, and analysis of marketing data and business needs. Others contributed to the development of the Raven application prototype and its predecessors: Bob Allen, Aruna Bayya, Nina Berry, Steve Bulick, Tony Cox, Simo El-Khadiri, Ed Freeman, Heidi Huber, Robert Joseph, Srdjan Kovacevic, Daniel Lin, Tim McCandless, Edwin Norton, Becky Root, Jill Schmidt, Loren Sylvan, and Dave Wroblewski.

Bibliography

[1] An object-oriented approach to medical process automation. *Electronic Documents*, 3(4):13–27.

[2] J. F. Allen. Maintaining knowledge about temporal intervals. *Communications of the ACM*, 26:832–843, 1983.

[3] ANSI. *X12 Standard, Subrelease 003041*. ANSI, Alexandria, VA, February 1994.

[4] American National Standards Institute (ANSI). ANSI X.392 (Data Encryption Algorithm). 1981.

[5] Richard H. Baker. *EDI, What Managers Need to Know About the Revolution in Business Communications*. TAB Books, Blue Ridge Summit, 1991.

[6] Michael S. Baum and Henry H. Perritt. *Electroni Contracting Publishing and EDI Law*. Wiley Law Publications, New York, NY, 1991.

[7] K. Kuhn M. Reichert T. Beuter and P. Dadam. An infrastructure for cooperation and communication in an advanced information system. In *Symposium on Computer Applications in Medical Care*, pages 519–523. AMIA Press, 1994.

[8] P. Bonissone and J. Stillman. A case study in integration of case based and temporal reasoning using cafe and tachyon. In *ARPA/RL Knowledge-Based Planning and Scheduling Workshop*, February 1994.

[9] A.H. Boss and J.B. Ritter. *Electronic Data Interchange Agreements A Guide and Sourcebook*. ICC, Paris, 1993.

[10] M. W. Bright, A. R. Hurson, S. Pakzad, and H. Sarma. The Summary Schemas Model — An Approach for Handling Multidatabases: Concept and Performance Analysis. In A. R. Hurson, M. W. Bright, and S. H. Pakzad, editors, *Multidatabase Systems*. IEEE Computer Society Press, Los Alamitos, Calif., 1993.

[11] BSR. Basic reference document. Technical report, August 1994.

[12] C. Ellis, G. Nutt. Modeling and Enactment of Workflow Systems. In *Application and Theory of Petri Nets*, pages 1–16. LNCS, Springer Verlag, 1993.

[13] CCITT. The Directory - Overview of Concepts, Models and Service. *CCITT*, 1988.

[14] TEDIS Commission of the European Communities. *The Legal Position of the Member States with Respect to Electronic Data Interchange.* 1989.

[15] TEDIS Commission of the European Communities. *Draft Commission Recommendation on a European Model EDI Agreement.* October 1994.

[16] PDES/STEP Committee. *STEP: Standard for the Exchange of Product Model Data.* ISO 10303, International Organization for Standardization, Geneva, 1994.

[17] D. Georgakopoulos, M. Hornick, A. Sheth. An Overview of Workflow Management: From Process Modeling to Workflow Automation Infrastructure. In *International Journal on Distributed and Parallel Databases*, 1994.

[18] D. Watne, P. Turney. *Auditing EDP Systems.* Prentice Hall, 1990.

[19] R.V. De Mulder, P. Kleve, and J. vander Wees. Adr in edi. *Law, Computers and Artificial Intelligence*, 4(1), 95.

[20] R. Arthur A. Deitsch and J. Stillman. Tachyon: A constraint-based temporal reasoning model and its implementation. *SIGART Bulletin*, 4(3), July 1993.

[21] Linda G. DeMichiel. Performing Operations over Mismatched Domains. In *Proc. 5th Int. Conf. on Data Engineering.* 36-45, 1989. Reprinted in *Multidatabase Systems*, A. R. Hurson, M. W. Bright and S. H. Pakzad, Ed.s, IEEE Computer Society Press, Los Alamitos, Calif., 1993.

[22] Lisa C. Donatini. BIG EDI for GE Aircraft Engines' Suppliers. *EDI World*, 4(10):20–22, October 1994.

[23] Nancy B. Lehrer et al. *Knowledge Representation Specification Language (KRSL) Manual Version 2.0.2.* ARPA/Rome Laboratory Planning and Scheduling Initiative, ISX Corporation (1994 email: try nlehrer@isx.com), 1993.

[24] A. Fischer. Electronic Document Authorization. In P. Schicker, E. Sterrerud, editor, *Message Handling Systems and Application Layer Communication Protocols: Proceedings of IFIP WG6.5 International Symposium.* North Holland, 1990.

[25] D. Gangopadhyah and P.Y.F. Wu. Adonis-a vision of the future. In *Symposium on Computer Applications in Medical Care*, pages 508–511. McGraw-Hill, Boston Spa, 1993.

[26] J. Geller, Y. Perl, P. Cannata, A. Sheth, and E. Neuhold. A case study of structural integration. In Yelena Yesha, editor, *Proc. CIKM-92, Conference on Information and Knowledge Management.* International society for Computers and Their Applications, Dept. of Computer Science, University of Maryland Baltimore County, 1992.

[27] Michael R. Genesereth and Richard E. Fikes. *Knowledge Interchange Format, Version 3.0 Reference Manual.* Computer Science Dept., Stanford University, Stanford, CA 94305, 1992. Logic Group Report Logic-92-1.

[28] P. Srinivasan G. Vignes C. Venable A. Hazelwood and T. Cade. From chart tracking to workflow management. In *Symposium on Computer Applications in Medical Care*, pages 884–887. AMIA Press, 1994.

[29] D. Georgakopoulos M. Hornick and A. Sheth. An overview of workflow management: From process modeling to workflow automation infrastructure. *Distributed and Parallel Databases*, 3(2), November 1994.

[30] J. Huet. Aspect juridiques de l'edi. *Recueil Dalloz Sirey*, 27, July 1991.

[31] Michael N. Huhns, Nigel Jacobs, Tomasz Ksiezyk andWei Mion Shen, Munindar P. Singh, and Philip E. Cannata. Plausible inferencing using extended composition. In Charles Petrie, editor, *Enterprise Integration Modeling. Proc. of the 1st Int. Conf.*, Cambridge, Mass., 1992. MT Press.

[32] U.N. International Telecommunication Union (ITU). *EDIFACT: United Nations Directories Electronic Data Interchange For Administration, Commerce and Transport. 1994 Draft.* International Telecommunication Union (ITU), Geneva, 1994.

[33] K. Hales, M. Laverty. *Workflow Management Software: the Business Opportunity.* Ovum, 1991.

[34] W. Kilian. Edi forschungsproject "eltrado" - juristische aspecte. *EM - Electronic Markets*, 1, April 1994.

[35] Kevin Knight and Steve K. Luk. Building a large-scale knowledge base for machine translation. In *Proc. AAAI-94*, pages 773–778, 1994.

[36] Valentine Korah. *An Introductory Guide to EEC Competition Law and Practice.* ESC Publishing Limited, Oxford, 1990.

[37] T. Koulopoulos and N. Palmer. Go with the flow. *PC Magazine*, 13(11):253–302, 1994.

[38] N. Krishnakumar and A. Sheth. Managing heterogeneous multi-system tasks to support enterprise-wide operations. *Distributed and Parallel Databases*, 3(2), November 1994.

[39] T.W. Malone K. Crowston J. Lee and B. Pentland. Tools for inventing organizations: Toward a handbook of organizational processes. In *Second IEEE Workshop on Enabling Technologies Infrastructure for Collaborative Enterprises.* IEEE Press, 1993.

[40] Fritz Lehmann, editor. *Semantic Networks in Artificial Intelligence.* Pergamon Press, Oxford, 1992. Also appeared as a special issue of *Computers & Mathematics with Applications*, Vol. 23, No.s 2-9, 1992.

[41] Fritz Lehmann. CCAT: The Current Status of the Conceptual Catalogue Group, with Proposals. In Gerard Ellis, editor, *Third Peirce Workshop, A Conceptual Graph Workbench.* ICCS-94, G. Ellis, RMIT, Melbourne, Australia (1994 email: ged@cs.rmit.edu.au), 1994.

[42] Fritz Lehmann and Anthony G. Cohn. The EGG/YOLK Reliability Hierarchy: Semantic Data Integration Using Sorts with Prototypes. In *Proc. CIKM-94, Third International ACM Conference on Information and Knowledge Management.* ACM Press, 1515 Broadway, New York, NY 10036, 1994.

[43] T.H. Cormen C.E. Leiserson and R.L. Rivest. *Introduction to Algorithms.* MIT Press, Cambridge, MA, 1990.

[44] Douglas B. Lenat and Ramanathan V. Guha. *Building Large Knowledge Based Systems.* Addison-Wesley, Reading, Mass., 1990.

[45] V. Lilley. Smoothing the Workflow. *Internal Auditing*, 1993.

[46] S. M. Matyas. Key Processing with Control Vectors. *Journal of Cryptology*, pages 113–135, 1991.

[47] Alexa McCray. *UMLS Semantic Network.* Office of Public Information, National Libray of Medicine, Bethesda, MD, 1994.

[48] A Mitrakas. *Ways to Draft An Interchange Agreement - Report No. WP 95.02.03, EURIDIS.* Erasmus University Rotterdam, 1995.

[49] ISO/IEC JTC1/SC21/WG3/CSMF N1781. *Preliminary Working Draft on Conceptual Schema Modelling Facility.* ISO/IEC, Project JTC1.21.63, 1994.

[50] Klaus-Dieter Naujok. Standards Update: X12 Tri-Semester Meeting, June 5-10, 1994, Dallas. *EDI World*, 4(9):35, September 1994.

[51] Elmasri & Navathe. *Fundamentals of Database Systems.* The Benjamin/Cummings Publishing Company, 1989.

[52] S. B. Navathe, R. Elmasri, and J. A. Larson. Integrating User Views in Database Design. *IEEE Computer*, 19(1):50–62, 1986.

[53] CompuLaw Newsletter. Admissibility of computer records as evidence. *CompuLaw Newsletter Butterworths*, 1(1), September 1994.

[54] National Bureau of Standards. Announcing the Data Encryption Standard. *FIPS Publication*, 46, 1977.

[55] Commission of the European Communities. *XIX Competition Policy Report.* 1989.

[56] P. Papanicolaou. *On the Limits of the Protective Intervention of the Judge in a Contract.* Ant. N. Saccoulas Publishers, Athens, 1991.

[57] K. R. Pemble. Regional health information networks: The wisconsin health information network, a case study. In *Symposium on Computer Applications in Medical Care*, pages 401–405. AMIA Press, 1994.

[58] Charles Petrie, editor. *Enterprise Integration Modeling. Proc. of the 1st Int. Conf.* MIT Press, Cambridge, Mass., 1992.

[59] M. Purser. *Secure Data Networking.* Artech House, 1993.

[60] R. L. Rivest, A. Shamir, L. Adleman. A Method for Obtaining Digital Signatures and Public-Key Cryptosystems. *Communications of the ACM*, 21(2):120–126, 1978.

[61] D.A. Pisanelli F. Ferri F.L. Ricci. An object-oriented tool for the generation and management of multimedia patient folders. In *Symposium on Computer Applications in Medical Care*, pages 524–528. AMIA Press, 1994.

[62] J. Ritter. Edi legal strategies: The aba model trading partner agreement. *EDI Forum*, 1990.

[63] G. Rounis. *Competition or Corperation.* Ant. N. Saccoulas Publishers, Athens, 1992.

[64] M. Rusinkiewicz and A. Sheth. Specification and execution of transactional workflows. In W. Kim, editor, *Modern Database Systems: The Object Model, Interoperability, and Beyond.* Addison-Wesley, 1994.

[65] S. Russell. Planning for the EDI of Tomorrow using Electronic Document Authorization. *IFIP TC11 Ninth International Conference on Information Security*, IFIP Transactions A-37:243–251, 1993.

[66] I. Schinas. *Protection of Competition.* Ant. N. Saccoulas Publishers, Athens, 1992.

[67] Stuart Shapiro, William J. Rapaport, Sung-Hye Cho, Joongmin Choi, Elissa Feit, Susan Haller, and Deepak Kumar. *A Dictionary of SNePS Case Frames.* Dept. of Computer Science, State University of New York at Buffalo, Buffalo, NY 14260, 1992-1994.

[68] D. Woelk P. Cannata M. Huhns W. Shen and C. Tomlinson. Using carnot for enterprise information integration. In *Second International Conference on Parallel and Distributed Information Systems*, pages 133–136, 1993.

[69] John F. Sowa. *Conceptual Structures: Information Processing in Mind and Machine.* Addison-Wesley, Reading, Mass., 1984.

[70] John F. Sowa, editor. *Principles of Semantic Networks: Explorations in the Representation of Knowledge.* Morgan Kaufmann, San Mateo, Cal., 1991.

[71] K. Steel. Another approach to standardising edi. *Electronic Markets*, 12, September 1994.

[72] Ken Steel. The electronic derivation of a basic sematic repository from the edifact directory. November 1994.

[73] Ken Steel. Matching functionality of interoperating applications: Another approach to edi standardisation. Technical report, 1994.

[74] Ken Steel. *Matching Functionality of Interoperating Applications: Another Approach to EDI Standardisation.* Department of Computer Science, Univ. of Melbourne, and as ISO/IEC JTC1/WG3 IT117/94, Committee Draft of MAY94 (email preprint), 1994.

[75] J. Stillman. An approach to spatio-temporal retrieval and reasoning. In *GIS '93*, November 1993.

[76] J. Stillman. Dual use applications of tachyon: From force structure modeling to manufacturing scheduling. In *Fourth Annual IEEE Dual Use Technologies & Applications Conference*, May 1994.

[77] C. Tapper. *Computer Law.* Longman, London, 1989.

[78] Basic Semantic Repository Prototype Team (Alan Thienot). *BSR (Basic Semantic Repository) Reference Document.* BSR/IMC/PPT/94N0022, ISO UN/ECE (email distribution, 7 Jul. 94), 1994.

[79] H.B. Thomsen and B.S. Wheble. *Trading with EDI: The Legal Issues.* IBC Financial Books Ltd., London, 1989.

[80] UN/EDIFACT. Application level syntax rules. Technical report, September 1994.

[81] Vincent Ventrone and Sandra Heiler. Semantic Heterogeneity as a Result of Domain Evolution. *SIGMOD Record*, 20(4):16–20, 1989. Reprinted in *Multidatabase Systems*, A. R. Hurson, M. W. Bright and S. H. Pakzad, Ed.s, IEEE Computer Society Press, Los Alamitos, Calif., 1993.

[82] W. Diffie, M.E. Hellman. New Directions in Cryptography. *IEEE Transactions on Information Theory*, IT-22:644–654, 1976.

[83] J. Webster. Edi: A pessimistic view. *EM - Electronic Markets*, 13-14, January 1995.

[84] E. Woolf. *Auditing Today.* Prentice Hall, 1990.

[85] B. Wright. *The Law of Electronic Commerce, EDI, Fax, e-mail.* Little-Brown and Co., Boston, 1991.

[86] B. Wright. Do we need trading partner agreements. *EDI Forum*, 7(1), 1994.

Lecture Notes in Computer Science

For information about Vols. 1–954

please contact your bookseller or Springer-Verlag

Vol. 955: S.G. Akl, F. Dehne, J.-R. Sack, N. Santoro (Eds.), Algorithms and Data Structures. Proceedings, 1995. IX, 519 pages. 1995.

Vol. 956: X. Yao (Ed.), Progress in Evolutionary Computation. Proceedings, 1993, 1994. VIII, 314 pages. 1995. (Subseries LNAI).

Vol. 957: C. Castelfranchi, J.-P. Müller (Eds.), From Reaction to Cognition. Proceedings, 1993. VI, 252 pages. 1995. (Subseries LNAI).

Vol. 958: J. Calmet, J.A. Campbell (Eds.), Integrating Symbolic Mathematical Computation and Artificial Intelligence. Proceedings, 1994. X, 275 pages. 1995.

Vol. 959: D.-Z. Du, M. Li (Eds.), Computing and Combinatorics. Proceedings, 1995. XIII, 654 pages. 1995.

Vol. 960: D. Leivant (Ed.), Logic and Computational Complexity. Proceedings, 1994. VIII, 514 pages. 1995.

Vol. 961: K.P. Jantke, S. Lange (Eds.), Algorithmic Learning for Knowledge-Based Systems. X, 511 pages. 1995. (Subseries LNAI).

Vol. 962: I. Lee, S.A. Smolka (Eds.), CONCUR '95: Concurrency Theory. Proceedings, 1995. X, 547 pages. 1995.

Vol. 963: D. Coppersmith (Ed.), Advances in Cryptology - CRYPTO '95. Proceedings, 1995. XII, 467 pages. 1995.

Vol. 964: V. Malyshkin (Ed.), Parallel Computing Technologies. Proceedings, 1995. XII, 497 pages. 1995.

Vol. 965: H. Reichel (Ed.), Fundamentals of Computation Theory. Proceedings, 1995. IX, 433 pages. 1995.

Vol. 966: S. Haridi, K. Ali, P. Magnusson (Eds.), EURO-PAR '95 Parallel Processing. Proceedings, 1995. XV, 734 pages. 1995.

Vol. 967: J.P. Bowen, M.G. Hinchey (Eds.), ZUM '95: The Z Formal Specification Notation. Proceedings, 1995. XI, 571 pages. 1995.

Vol. 968: N. Dershowitz, N. Lindenstrauss (Eds.), Conditional and Typed Rewriting Systems. Proceedings, 1994. VIII, 375 pages. 1995.

Vol. 969: J. Wiedermann, P. Hájek (Eds.), Mathematical Foundations of Computer Science 1995. Proceedings, 1995. XIII, 588 pages. 1995.

Vol. 970: V. Hlaváč, R. Šára (Eds.), Computer Analysis of Images and Patterns. Proceedings, 1995. XVIII, 960 pages. 1995.

Vol. 971: E.T. Schubert, P.J. Windley, J. Alves-Foss (Eds.), Higher Order Logic Theorem Proving and Its Applications. Proceedings, 1995. VIII, 400 pages. 1995.

Vol. 972: J.-M. Hélary, M. Raynal (Eds.), Distributed Algorithms. Proceedings, 1995. XI, 333 pages. 1995.

Vol. 973: H.H. Adelsberger, J. Lažanský, V. Mařík (Eds.), Information Management in Computer Integrated Manufacturing. IX, 665 pages. 1995.

Vol. 974: C. Braccini, L. DeFloriani, G. Vernazza (Eds.), Image Analysis and Processing. Proceedings, 1995. XIX, 757 pages. 1995.

Vol. 975: W. Moore, W. Luk (Eds.), Field-Programmable Logic and Applications. Proceedings, 1995. XI, 448 pages. 1995.

Vol. 976: U. Montanari, F. Rossi (Eds.), Principles and Practice of Constraint Programming — CP '95. Proceedings, 1995. XIII, 651 pages. 1995.

Vol. 977: H. Beilner, F. Bause (Eds.), Quantitative Evaluation of Computing and Communication Systems. Proceedings, 1995. X, 415 pages. 1995.

Vol. 978: N. Revell, A M. Tjoa (Eds.), Database and Expert Systems Applications. Proceedings, 1995. XV, 654 pages. 1995.

Vol. 979: P. Spirakis (Ed.), Algorithms — ESA '95. Proceedings, 1995. XII, 598 pages. 1995.

Vol. 980: A. Ferreira, J. Rolim (Eds.), Parallel Algorithms for Irregularly Structured Problems. Proceedings, 1995. IX, 409 pages. 1995.

Vol. 981: I. Wachsmuth, C.-R. Rollinger, W. Brauer (Eds.), KI-95: Advances in Artificial Intelligence. Proceedings, 1995. XII, 269 pages. (Subseries LNAI).

Vol. 982: S. Doaitse Swierstra, M. Hermenegildo (Eds.), Programming Languages: Implementations, Logics and Programs. Proceedings, 1995. XI, 467 pages. 1995.

Vol. 983: A. Mycroft (Ed.), Static Analysis. Proceedings, 1995. VIII, 423 pages. 1995.

Vol. 984: J.-M. Haton, M. Keane, M. Manago (Eds.), Advances in Case-Based Reasoning. Proceedings, 1994. VIII, 307 pages. 1995.

Vol. 985: T. Sellis (Ed.), Rules in Database Systems. Proceedings, 1995. VIII, 373 pages. 1995.

Vol. 986: Henry G. Baker (Ed.), Memory Management. Proceedings, 1995. XII, 417 pages. 1995.

Vol. 987: P.E. Camurati, H. Eveking (Eds.), Correct Hardware Design and Verification Methods. Proceedings, 1995. VIII, 342 pages. 1995.

Vol. 988: A.U. Frank, W. Kuhn (Eds.), Spatial Information Theory. Proceedings, 1995. XIII, 571 pages. 1995.

Vol. 989: W. Schäfer, P. Botella (Eds.), Software Engineering — ESEC '95. Proceedings, 1995. XII, 519 pages. 1995.

Vol. 990: C. Pinto-Ferreira, N.J. Mamede (Eds.), Progress in Artificial Intelligence. Proceedings, 1995. XIV, 487 pages. 1995. (Subseries LNAI).

Vol. 991: J. Wainer, A. Carvalho (Eds.), Advances in Artificial Intelligence. Proceedings, 1995. XII, 342 pages. 1995. (Subseries LNAI).

Vol. 992: M. Gori, G. Soda (Eds.), Topics in Artificial Intelligence. Proceedings, 1995. XII, 451 pages. 1995. (Subseries LNAI).

Vol. 993: T.C. Fogarty (Ed.), Evolutionary Computing. Proceedings, 1995. VIII, 264 pages. 1995.

Vol. 994: M. Hebert, J. Ponce, T. Boult, A. Gross (Eds.), Object Representation in Computer Vision. Proceedings, 1994. VIII, 359 pages. 1995.

Vol. 995: S.M. Müller, W.J. Paul, The Complexity of Simple Computer Architectures. XII, 270 pages. 1995.

Vol. 996: P. Dybjer, B. Nordström, J. Smith (Eds.), Types for Proofs and Programs. Proceedings, 1994. X, 202 pages. 1995.

Vol. 997: K.P. Jantke, T. Shinohara, T. Zeugmann (Eds.), Algorithmic Learning Theory. Proceedings, 1995. XV, 319 pages. 1995.

Vol. 998: A. Clarke, M. Campolargo, N. Karatzas (Eds.), Bringing Telecommunication Services to the People – IS&N '95. Proceedings, 1995. XII, 510 pages. 1995.

Vol. 999: P. Antsaklis, W. Kohn, A. Nerode, S. Sastry (Eds.), Hybrid Systems II. VIII, 569 pages. 1995.

Vol. 1000: J. van Leeuwen (Ed.), Computer Science Today. XIV, 643 pages. 1995.

Vol. 1001: M. Sudan, Efficient Checking of Polynomials and Proofs and the Hardness of Approximation Problems. XIV, 87 pages. 1995.

Vol. 1002: J.J. Kistler, Disconnected Operation in a Distributed File System. XIX, 249 pages. 1995.

VOL. 1003: P. Pandurang Nayak, Automated Modeling of Physical Systems. XXI, 232 pages. 1995. (Subseries LNAI).

Vol. 1004: J. Staples, P. Eades, N. Katoh, A. Moffat (Eds.), Algorithms and Computation. Proceedings, 1995. XV, 440 pages. 1995.

Vol. 1005: J. Estublier (Ed.), Software Configuration Management. Proceedings, 1995. IX, 311 pages. 1995.

Vol. 1006: S. Bhalla (Ed.), Information Systems and Data Management. Proceedings, 1995. IX, 321 pages. 1995.

Vol. 1007: A. Bosselaers, B. Preneel (Eds.), Integrity Primitives for Secure Information Systems. VII, 239 pages. 1995.

Vol. 1008: B. Preneel (Ed.), Fast Software Encryption. Proceedings, 1994. VIII, 367 pages. 1995.

Vol. 1009: M. Broy, S. Jähnichen (Eds.), KORSO: Methods, Languages, and Tools for the Construction of Correct Software. X, 449 pages. 1995. Vol.

Vol. 1010: M. Veloso, A. Aamodt (Eds.), Case-Based Reasoning Research and Development. Proceedings, 1995. X, 576 pages. 1995. (Subseries LNAI).

Vol. 1011: T. Furuhashi (Ed.), Advances in Fuzzy Logic, Neural Networks and Genetic Algorithms. Proceedings, 1994. (Subseries LNAI).

Vol. 1012: M. Bartošek, J. Staudek, J. Wiedermann (Eds.), SOFSEM '95: Theory and Practice of Informatics. Proceedings, 1995. XI, 499 pages. 1995.

Vol. 1013: T.W. Ling, A.O. Mendelzon, L. Vieille (Eds.), Deductive and Object-Oriented Databases. Proceedings, 1995. XIV, 557 pages. 1995.

Vol. 1014: A.P. del Pobil, M.A. Serna, Spatial Representation and Motion Planning. XII, 242 pages. 1995.

Vol. 1015: B. Blumenthal, J. Gornostaev, C. Unger (Eds.), Human-Computer Interaction. Proceedings, 1995. VIII, 203 pages. 1995.

VOL. 1016: R. Cipolla, Active Visual Inference of Surface Shape. XII, 194 pages. 1995.

Vol. 1017: M. Nagl (Ed.), Graph-Theoretic Concepts in Computer Science. Proceedings, 1995. XI, 406 pages. 1995.

Vol. 1018: T.D.C. Little, R. Gusella (Eds.), Network and Operating Systems Support for Digital Audio and Video. Proceedings, 1995. XI, 357 pages. 1995.

Vol. 1019: E. Brinksma, W.R. Cleaveland, K.G. Larsen, T. Margaria, B. Steffen (Eds.), Tools and Algorithms for the Construction and Analysis of Systems. Selected Papers, 1995. VII, 291 pages. 1995.

Vol. 1020: I.D. Watson (Ed.), Progress in Case-Based Reasoning. Proceedings, 1995. VIII, 209 pages. 1995. (Subseries LNAI).

Vol. 1021: M.P. Papazoglou (Ed.), OOER '95: Object-Oriented and Entity-Relationship Modeling. Proceedings, 1995. XVII, 451 pages. 1995.

Vol. 1022: P.H. Hartel, R. Plasmeijer (Eds.), Functional Programming Languages in Education. Proceedings, 1995. X, 309 pages. 1995.

Vol. 1023: K. Kanchanasut, J.-J. Lévy (Eds.), Algorithms, Concurrency and Knowlwdge. Proceedings, 1995. X, 410 pages. 1995.

Vol. 1024: R.T. Chin, H.H.S. Ip, A.C. Naiman, T.-C. Pong (Eds.), Image Analysis Applications and Computer Graphics. Proceedings, 1995. XVI, 533 pages. 1995.

Vol. 1025: C. Boyd (Ed.), Cryptography and Coding. Proceedings, 1995. IX, 291 pages. 1995.

Vol. 1026: P.S. Thiagarajan (Ed.), Foundations of Software Technology and Theoretical Computer Science. Proceedings, 1995. XII, 515 pages. 1995.

Vol. 1027: F.J. Brandenburg (Ed.), Graph Drawing. Proceedings, 1995. XII, 526 pages. 1996.

Vol. 1028: N.R. Adam, Y. Yesha (Eds.), Electronic Commerce. X, 155 pages. 1996.

Vol. 1029: E. Dawson, J. Golić (Eds.), Cryptography: Policy and Algorithms. Proceedings, 1995. XI, 327 pages. 1996.

Vol. 1030: F. Pichler, R. Moreno-Díaz, R. Albrecht (Eds.), Computer Aided Systems Theory - EUROCAST '95. Proceedings, 1995. XII, 539 pages. 1996.

Vol.1031: M. Toussaint (Ed.), Ada in Europe. Proceedings, 1995. XI, 455 pages. 1996.

Vol. 1032: P. Godefroid, Partial-Order Methods for the Verification of Concurrent Systems. IV, 143 pages. 1996.

www.ingramcontent.com/pod-product-compliance
Lightning Source LLC
Chambersburg PA
CBHW070026240926
52026CB00005B/163
* 9 7 8 3 5 4 0 6 0 7 3 8 0 *